Girl Uprooted

LENA LEE

LITTLE KOO PRESS

First published by Little Koo Press in 2023

Copyright © Lena Lee, 2023

Lena Lee asserts the moral right to be identified
as the author of this work.

This book is a work of non-fiction.
Some names and identifying characteristics have been
changed to protect the privacy of others.

Caution: this book contains references to depression,
addiction, eating disorders and suicide.

ISBN (PB) 978-1-7394171-0-9
ISBN (E) 978-1-7394171-1-6

"A tree with strong roots does not suffer from drought."

KOREAN PROVERB

Contents

Contents

Introduction

When people ask me where I am from, my response is qualified with, "I'm Korean, but…" I can't really get away with, "I'm Korean, full stop," because of my funny international accent, so I usually go with the short answer: "…but I moved around a lot."

The conversation either stops there—with a blank stare—or leads to the next question: "Oh, where have you lived?"

There are a few variations to this, but sometimes I might challenge them to remember the sequence of countries I have lived in. "Okay, you ready?" I say, then reel off, "Born in Korea, then moved to the US, Korea, Malaysia, the US"—I've usually lost them by this point—"Korea, France, then the UK and Norway. Got it?"

"Wow, how many languages do you speak? What's your favorite country? You must have friends all over the world!"

I smile weakly because I don't really know what to say, or where to start. The truth is, my entire life was upended every three years. With one flight, everything changed: not only my house, school and friends, but the food, the language, the culture, the climate, the color of people's skins. *Everything*. And with each move, I had to relearn the "right" way to

1

think and talk and eat and dress and study and play. My mom would praise me for how well I adapted and how easily I made friends in each country—as if I had a choice.

Fitting in was a survival skill. To paraphrase Darwin, it's not the most intellectual or the strongest that survive, but the ones best able to adapt and adjust to a changing environment. And change it did. It was only a matter of time before the constant shapeshifting caught up with me.

After attending university in the UK, I returned to Korea in 2013 at the age of twenty-two. Korea was supposed to be my home—well, I was born there, I looked Korean, I spoke Korean, all my extended family lived there—but I didn't *feel* Korean. No, Korea couldn't be my home. But then, where was?

It hit me only then that I was no longer the daughter of a diplomat, an identity I was born with and one that had shaped my whole life. In fact, moving countries every few years had been the only way of life I knew; it was just the way it was. Now, I no longer had a diplomatic passport and needed a visa to live in any other country. But as much as I rejected Korea, and felt rejected by it, I didn't seem to belong anywhere else.

And rather than having friends all over the world, I felt like I didn't have friends *anywhere* in the world. After repeating the cycle of making friends then saying goodbye one too many times, it simply became too painful to invest in friendships.

The only meaningful constants in my life were my mom, dad and brother (and our Yorkshire Terrier). But aside from a generational gap, I felt a language barrier—maybe it wasn't so much a barrier as an awkwardness—and an insurmountable cultural gap with my parents, especially my dad, who had been born and raised in Korea in a very different time. It would only be as an adult that I would start to understand the vast differences in our education, upbringing and values.

Today, at thirty-two years old, I have been living in London for nine years, by far the longest continuous period I have lived anywhere; yet it is no easier now to answer the question, "Where are you from?"

And although I am bilingual in English and Korean, I am not a native speaker of either. In English, I say things like "toe thumb" (instead of big toe), which is how you say it in Korean, and my Korean is slipping away with every year I live "abroad." I don't know if this explains why, for so many years, I didn't feel like I had the words to express myself, but now, through writing, I have come to be at home with my in-betweenness.

This is my story of being uprooted many times over and finding a sense of identity, belonging and home.

PART ONE

The Ambassador's Daughter

2010–2013

1

OSLO, NORWAY, 2010 (age 19)

It wasn't difficult to spot my parents among a pool of Norwegians as I wheeled my suitcase out of Rygge, Oslo's low-cost airport. It was my first time visiting from Oxford University, where I'd recently started studying, and my backpack was heavy with books for my course. As I gave my mom a hug and my dad an awkward smile, a small Filipino man rushed over to relieve me of my luggage. With a warm smile, Dodong introduced himself as our driver and opened the doors to the shiny black Hyundai Equus, the official state car of Korea, parked outside. The license plate was marked CD for *Corps Diplomatique*. My dad gave up his seat so I could sit in the back with my mom.

"Residence, Sir?" Dodong asked.

A nod.

"Yes, Sir." And off we went.

Out the window, the highway gave way to central Oslo, which seemed remarkably tranquil for a capital city, certainly without any of the hustle and bustle of Seoul. Everyone looked like models—tall, blond and beautiful.

"I bet we look like penguins to them," I said.

"Hah, waddling around with our short little legs." My mom and I often made self-deprecating jokes like this.

Outside the house, we waited for the wrought iron gates to open. They were painted with the red-and-blue yin-yang symbol from the South Korean flag. Past the gates, an actual flag waved up high from a white post. We were being watched by a CCTV camera. I'd had many, many homes over the years but none called the "Official Residence of the Ambassador of the Republic of Korea" as the golden plaque outside read.

Through the gates, we drove up a short, steep incline to a modern two-story house with floor-to-ceiling windows. As I stepped into the double-height foyer lit by a chandelier, a middle-aged woman in an apron jumped out to greet me. It was our chef. I bowed respectfully and said, "*Annyounghaseyo*." She too bowed and greeted me in the honorific form even though I was half her age.

"Lena, you're here!" Our cleaner was the only familiar face in Norway apart from my parents. She used to help a few times a week at our previous posting in Paris and had been happy to relocate when my dad was reassigned. She was *Joseonjok*, an ethnic Korean born and raised in China, so she spoke Korean fluently, though she said some words differently. She'd been a primary school teacher back in China but had emigrated to France, leaving behind her daughter for better wages.

"It's good to see you here, Ajumma," I said, and squeezed her tight. She insisted we call her *ajumma*, a term which used to be commonly adopted for married or middle-aged women—I called my mom's friends *ajumma* growing up—

but was falling out of fashion. She called me by name as a sign of familiarity but spoke to me in the polite form as a show of respect.

Afraid of missing out, our Yorkshire Terrier, Jjanga, came out barking and wagging her tail. (Her name is pronounced with a harsh J sound that is difficult to pronounce for Westerners, though she would not have deigned to respond to anything mispronounced like "Jenga.") Jjanga seemed nicely settled into her new Scandinavian life after my parents had driven her twenty hours from France, through Belgium, Germany and Denmark, as well as taking a ferry to Sweden, to avoid the strict quarantine rules in Norway. Jjanga was family, though. We got her when I was six and this was already her fifth international move.

Dodong delivered my bags to what would be my room. I followed him up the bright red carpeted staircase and quickly unpacked my things—there wasn't a huge amount anyway.

Back downstairs, my dad popped open a bottle of Veuve Clicquot, his favorite champagne, and mine too. "Welcome to my humble abode," he said. He loved using expressions like this, ones that he'd picked up on TV and studiously looked up. As I gazed around the marble walls, the celadon vases and the miniature flags of Korea and Norway crisscrossed against each other, my dad eagerly explained that the house had been built in the late sixties by a famous architect and that the original owner had been a playboy before it somehow ended up in the hands of the Korean government. Indeed, the basement bar looked more appropriate for a frat party than for foreign dignitaries. Now, the house was marked with the distinct and eclectic tastes of our various predecessors. My mom, too, would leave behind her imprint when the budget was replenished, allowing her to order new curtains and furniture.

This would be my new home, for the time being, as was the way.

Besides these luxuries afforded to the ambassador, my parents would enjoy many other perks. They would make annual trips to Reykjavik for the Icelandic National Day celebrations. They would visit Svalbard, a Norwegian archipelago in the Arctic Ocean where road signs warn of polar bears and you are not permitted to leave the settlement without a gun. They would see the fjords and the northern lights and meet the nomadic, reindeer-herding Sami. They would attend the Nobel Peace Prize ceremony each year. My mom would even get to take a photo with Denzel Washington, her all-time favorite actor, at the first ceremony. (Unfortunately, there were no Hollywood actors present the year I tagged along. The European Union won that year, and I only got to see how tiny Angela Merkel is in person.)

I suppose this is the kind of thing people imagine about the diplomatic lifestyle, but my dad had been some twenty-five years in the diplomatic service before he became an ambassador. Unlike in some other countries where senior diplomats can be political appointees, Korean ambassadors are all career diplomats. My dad had to work his way up the pecking order, from Second Secretary, First Secretary, Counselor, Minister-Counselor to Minister and only then, Ambassador.

In 1987, a few years before I was born, my dad, then a junior diplomat, was sent to Rwanda. His mission was to open the South Korean embassy as part of the government's efforts to be admitted to the United Nations. The Cold War was on and Kim Il-sung, the founding father of North Korea, was busy advancing the communist cause in Africa with money and weapons. South Korea felt it had to establish a counter-presence. (South Korea had, in fact, opened the first embassy back in 1972 but closed it three years later, miffed that the Rwandan government remained friendly with North Korea.)

Although hardship posts are a rite of passage for diplomats, my mom says my dad's face blanched upon hearing their next destination. Not only was Rwanda one of the poorest countries in Africa but it also had a high prevalence of HIV, though it wasn't understood at the time how the disease spread. After all, this was in the late eighties when the AIDS epidemic was just entering public awareness in the US. My parents would belatedly receive an apology from the resourcing department responsible for their assignment to Rwanda—if only they'd known about the baby. My brother was just a few months old.

Based on the albums my mom put together—now fading photos glued on flimsy paper—their life back then looks idyllic. They live in a spacious five-bed, two-story house, which is protected by a reed gate. The rooms are painted in a pinkish tone you might find in a grimy motel, but there is a chandelier in the dining room and an incongruous pair of banana leaf chairs in the sitting room. Beyond bananas, pineapples and papayas, which were plentiful year-round, food was scarce, so they planted fruits and vegetables, including strawberries and cabbages, in their garden. Lacking in provisions, my mom looked forward to the goodies her mother sent her from Korea via diplomatic pouches every two weeks.

There are photos of my mom, dad and brother all wearing matching clothes made from the same tropical print, which my mom sewed herself. She also acted as their barber, draping a towel around my dad and brother in turns and improvising with a pair of scissors on the balcony. They owned a television but could only play videotapes on it. Rwanda was one of the few countries at the time without a television network, which my mom tells me somewhat boastfully now.

My parents employed four Rwandan helpers—a cleaner, a driver, a babysitter and a gardener-cum-night guard— who mostly commuted barefoot to save money on shoes. My mom once took my brother and his babysitter Clotilde, whom my brother called Canna, to a function held at a fancy hotel. Canna pulled my mom aside and, pointing to a door that kept opening and closing, asked, "What's in that small room?" She had never seen an elevator before.

My parents and brother went on road trips within Rwanda and to neighboring Burundi and Uganda, often driving on treacherous dirt roads. There are photos of them sticking their heads out the sunroof of their Mercedes, with wildlife in the background. My mom says coolly that impalas, zebras and baboons were so common they scarcely bothered stopping for them.

One time they went to visit the Maasai village in Kenya where the local tribe wore ornate beaded jewelry and had enormous ear piercings. As pastoralists, they wielded wooden sticks and lived in circular huts plastered with cow dung: cracked, but sturdy. My parents were fascinated by their customs and politely asked to take photos with them. For the Maasai, my brother was as much of a spectacle. They were used to seeing Westerners but very few Asians. They huddled around my brother, wanting to stroke his silky black hair and soft skin, a heartwarming moment of mutual intrigue.

Unfortunately, the situation was about to turn dark in Rwanda. In October 1990, the rebels invaded the country from their base in neighboring Uganda to overthrow the president. The rebels were mostly Tutsi refugees who had been the wealthier and dominant minority in Rwanda until the country became a Hutu-dominated state following independence from Belgium in 1962. After the invasion, a dusk-to-dawn curfew was imposed. For expats, dinner parties became sleepovers. My brother, of course, managed to fall and gash his eyebrow one evening after curfew. My parents had to mount the Korean flag on their car before driving him to the emergency room as if for a state visit.

Then came rumblings of an attack in Kigali, the capital city. On the day of the attack, my mom was warned by a friend who she played tennis with and whose husband was a senior official in the French military. She relayed the message to my dad, who had his own intelligence from the American embassy and dismissed the rumors. "That's nonsense," he said. Sure enough, there was an attack that night: a reminder to never underestimate a woman's intelligence.

Next door to my parents lived a Tutsi bigwig, and shots were fired, or misfired, at their house. To use a Korean idiom, it was a shrimp getting hurt in a whale fight. My parents crawled and hid in the corridor, away from the windows, to dodge the bullets. "Tuck your butt in!" my mom shouted. Unlike my toddler brother, my dad was unwieldy on all fours. When the gunshots became louder, they crept to the bathroom, which was in a more secluded part of the house. After putting up mattresses against the window, they took cover until the morning. Windows were shattered overnight. My brother whined that he wanted to play, but in the playroom his toys were mixed with shards of glass.

By the time the gunfight broke out, two of my dad's colleagues had left the country and he became the chargé d'affaires. While diplomats and other expats were offered flights out of the country, the local population, of course, had no such privilege to flee. My mom, now five months pregnant with me, took safety in Kenya with my brother, who was three then, and called her mother for advice. Thinking back to the time when families were separated during the Korean War, my grandma warned my mom not to get separated from her husband: "No matter what, don't come back until your family is together." So, my mom waited in Kenya to be reunited with my dad and they returned to Korea together in December 1990. I was born four months later.

My dad is not a natural storyteller but this was a well-worn tale he knew how to tell with the right amount of drama and anticipation. "Bang! Bang! Bang!" Eyes wide, he would mimic the gunshots and impersonate my mom's shouts as dinner party guests glanced over at her in amazement. What I realized recently, though, is that my dad wasn't telling this story purely for entertainment. By recalling this incident, I think he was also reminding himself of how far he'd come.

I forget sometimes that my dad had a very different upbringing to mine, and that the Korea he grew up in was unrecognizable from the one I would experience. He was born in 1957, only a few years after the Korean War, when they say the country was as poor as Ghana. Following the war, Korea was a major recipient of foreign aid, notably from the UN World Food Programme (WFP), the humanitarian organization I'd always associated with efforts to combat famine in regions like Africa and the Middle East. But it wasn't just food assistance the country needed. The UN Korean Reconstruction Agency (UNKRA) was established to help with everything from housing and health to industry and irrigation—the rebuilding of an entire nation. However, within a generation, Korea transitioned from being a recipient to a donor country. Now rice bags stamped with the Korean flag are delivered to vulnerable people around the world, and South Korea has a seat at the "rich countries' club," the Organization for Economic Cooperation and Development (OECD).

This spectacular transformation has been described as the Miracle on the Han, the river that flows through Seoul. It was less a miracle than a series of economic and political reforms (by an authoritarian regime with a questionable human rights record) and a lot of hard work. Koreans are acutely aware of the lack of natural resources on our tiny peninsula, hence the need to rely on our brains, and hence the education fever, which I would experience first-hand.

My dad grew up in a small fishing village called Jangheung in southernmost Korea. (I only learned this recently in the process of fact-checking this book. I'd thought he'd grown up in Gunsan, which turns out to be the village they only moved to much later in life.) My dad was not the eldest—he has an older sister—but he was, crucially, the eldest son. He was smart and industrious as a student and went to a competitive boarding school in Gwangju, 80 kilometers north of his hometown. If he ever tried to visit home during term, his mother—my grandmother, who I called Gunsan *halmoni* after the village—would come at him with a broom, shouting in her strong dialect, "What you doing wasting your time? Go study!" He was accepted to Seoul National University, the Harvard of Korea, where he majored in French, one of the two working languages of the United Nations, then became the second youngest person to pass the notoriously challenging foreign service exam.

It is only now that I appreciate what a remarkable achievement that is. My dad was not born with a silver spoon. He came from humble beginnings and had to work for everything he achieved. As ambassador, he was finally at the pinnacle of his decades-long foreign-service career. It was everything he had worked for. He relished his new title, "Ambassador Lee," and loved opening invitations addressed to "His Excellency" and everything that entailed. He proudly displayed his photos with King Harald V, taken when he was invited to the Royal Palace to be formally accredited to Norway.

And here I was, living in this grand residence with a chef and a live-in cleaner, being treated with great respect as the ambassador's daughter.

Growing up, my dad would drone on to me and my brother about the importance of possessing a "hungry" mentality and the need to be more "spartan" (he'd pronounce these words with a thick Korean accent: "hung-geu-ree" and "spa-roo-tahn").

He liked to remind us, "What are the five Confucian relationships?" When he elicited no response from either of us—other than an eye roll—he'd shout, "Seung Gon!"

My brother would then half-heartedly recite, "Father to son, elder to younger brother, husband to wife, emperor to subject, and friend to friend."

"That's right, what's the first one?"

"Yeah, yeah, filial piety, I get it."

Hyodo. I hated it when my dad brought up these stupid old-fashioned values. You couldn't just demand respect and obedience, even from your own children. You earned respect—not with your title or status, but with love and warmth.

I didn't want a father who was just a provider and an authority figure. I wanted a dad who doted on me, like one of those "*ddal babo*" fathers—a daughter's fool.

2

My mom met my dad in 1985 on a blind date arranged by her mother's friend, a distant relative of my dad's. She had just graduated from Ewha Womans University with a degree in English Literature, cream of the crop in her generation. She was brought up in Seoul in a well-to-do family, her father a prominent doctor. My dad, already in the foreign service, was due to start his first overseas posting soon and insisted they get married after just a few dates so she could come with him. She said yes.

It's very difficult for me to imagine my parents passionately in love. They are not the lovey-dovey kind, ones to kiss or say "I love you" in front of me; I doubt they do so even in private. But they look happy in their wedding photos, my mom still chubby-cheeked and my dad's jaw chiseled. The guests are not smiling, as was the custom at the time—a wedding was a solemn event symbolizing the woman being passed over to the husband's household. My mom, though, has a carefree, innocent smile.

At the end of the album, there are photos of what look like a wedding reception. My mom is dressed up in a brown velour skirt suit with a flamboyant yellow brooch and white stilettos. My dad is in a suit and tie. My grandma and great-grandma are wearing their long, silky, traditional *hanbok* costumes and holding clutch bags. My mom's friends and my dad's sisters are all suited up too. But the venue seems slightly off for a reception and the mood too somber. It turns out these photos were taken at the airport. Just five days after the wedding, the newlyweds left for Portugal, my dad's first assignment. They stopped over in Paris for their honeymoon.

"Umma, isn't this a bit over the top?" I ask. I would normally wear sweatpants and a hoodie to the airport.

"Foreign travel was a big deal at the time, you know," my mom says. "It was only liberalized in the eighties."

"What do you mean 'liberalized'?"

"It was unthinkable to go abroad before then," she explains. "You needed a valid reason, not just some vacation."

I suspect my mom is exaggerating and check Naver, the Korean Google. But she's right. Until the eighties, passport issues were tightly controlled by the Korean government to prevent a foreign currency drain, as well as any contact with communist countries.

"When did you first go abroad?" I ask, still incredulous.

"My senior year of college, we went to Japan."

"And Appa?"

"Your dad went for his apprenticeship in France, so he must have been twenty-five."

"Oh." I never knew this, that my dad had never set foot outside Korea when he dreamed of becoming a globe-trotting diplomat.

18

Six years younger than my dad, my mom was only twenty-two when she walked down the aisle. I sometimes wonder if what she really wanted wasn't so much to get married but to start a new life, to be whisked away to foreign lands. In that way, setting aside other faults in the union, she found her perfect match in marrying a diplomat.

The best way to describe my mom is as a permanent cultural exchange student, ready to absorb as much as she can. She loves meeting new people, trying new foods and learning new languages. When I was around nine and living in Malaysia, my mom took me to the Batu Caves during the Thaipusam festival, which is celebrated by the local Hindu Tamil community. It was a pure assault on the senses: new sights, smells and sounds. Beneath the chanting and drumming, we were surrounded by Hindu men and women wearing marigold garlands around their necks, bright yellow and orange and red everywhere. There weren't many outsiders like us, so we immediately stood out. I held my mom's hand tight as we weaved through women balancing silver milk pots on their heads and men carrying elaborate structures on their shoulders. I remember complaining about the overpowering smell of incense and my mom scolding me for holding my nose. But most vivid in my memories are the hooks and skewers piercing through tongues and cheeks. There were men with metal hooks dangling all over their backs; some had ornaments and fruit weighing on those hooks; others had ropes attached to those hooks, and I could see their skin being tugged and stretched; still others were walking over hot coals. My mom was entirely in her element.

Although my mom had no formal title, her career as a trailing spouse mirrored my dad's, her social status in diplomatic circles being determined by his rank. Over the years, she did her fair share of kowtowing to the various Korean ambassadors' wives in respective countries, some notoriously catty and demanding. My mom now looked the part as the ambassador's wife: elegant and gracious. Her school friends call her the Korean Marilyn Monroe thanks to her signature hairstyle, which she coifs each morning with pink plastic hair rollers. My mom is also a people person, not in the overtly extroverted way but someone who can ingratiate herself easily and find a kindred spirit in anyone. To foreigners, she cutely introduces herself as "Kee Young, as in the key to being young." It's lucky she does look young.

My mom took her new role seriously. While my dad may have been the official host, the real burden of entertaining fell on her as the spouse. Her attention to detail started from brainstorming the menu: maybe something mild for foreigners trying Korean food for the first time, or something a little more adventurous for those who knew their favorite dishes; had the guests been invited before, what were they served last time? To buy the freshest ingredients, my mom would go to each of the butcher, the wholesale fish market, the local Rema grocery chain and the Asian supermarket. She liked to be hands-on in the kitchen, which occasionally led to some tension with the chef. My mom did not tolerate shortcuts—in cooking or in life. In preparation for parties, she would stay up late doing the flower arrangements herself, with her reading glasses on. She was not paid to do any of this—the government relies a great deal on the goodwill of the spouses—but my mom always liked to give it her best no matter what it was.

Whenever we hosted, my dad liked to take ceremonial photos on his phone (always a Samsung Galaxy; never an iPhone) with the guests, some at the dining table, others outside the front door with the South Korean emblem in the background. He would follow up afterwards with an email like this:

Thank you for your time with us today. It was a great pleasure to have a chat with you and your colleagues during humble luncheon at my residence. As we witness your knowledge about Korean cuisine and your skill how to use chopsticks, we'll prepare spicier kimchi next time.

Chopsticks and kimchi were easy conversation topics. We always served a side of kimchi and laid the table with a set of spoon and chopsticks, as well as a knife and fork for our Western guests to save them from any potential embarrassment. Korean chopsticks are particularly tricky to use because they are flat and made of metal, though most guests would at least make an attempt. Some would ask us the correct way to hold them; I always felt like a fraud giving the demonstration. As part of my holiday homework when I was seven or so and living in Korea, we had to transport a bowl of peas—pea by pea—using our chopsticks. Another task was to peel off layers of perilla leaf kimchi, which stick together into sheets. The trick was to pick up each leaf by the stem. I clearly didn't follow the instructions because I

21

still don't hold my chopsticks the "right" way, the kind of thing a Korean mother-in-law would tut at, not that the foreigners I was teaching noticed. Invariably, there would be a plop and a splatter as we put on a smile and tried to pretend it's not a pain in the ass to remove kimchi stains from a white tablecloth.

My dad could be charming when he wanted to be—when he felt the guests were important enough—but socializing didn't come so naturally to him. When we had Norwegian guests over, he would ask about the local history, with a particular interest in polar exploration. He wanted to know the details: the specific years of the expeditions, the names of the ships, the number of dogs that set off, the number of dogs that made it back. He would look these facts up afterwards, then when we had Korean guests over, he would tell them detailed stories about the explorers Nansen and Amundsen, hoping to impress with his wealth of local knowledge.

Sometimes my dad's efforts were lost in translation. For instance, he would declare at a dinner party, "My wife is not a great cook as you'll see, but I hope you'll enjoy the food anyway." This is a somewhat acceptable thing to say in Korea, where it is frowned upon to openly praise your spouse and say things like "my beautiful wife." Norwegians, however, are a people whose egalitarian values are literally codified in a set of ten rules called the Law of Jante. The first rule: "You are not to think you are anything special." What my dad means to do is invite even higher praise for my mom. In his own way, he is trying to be humble as he was taught to be. But he is oblivious to the way it comes across.

When my dad had to give a speech in English, he would practice out loud at home. He had a decent vocabulary—this was something he could rote learn—but his pronunciation was something that didn't improve in tandem with his efforts. He had a classic Korean accent and struggled with his Rs. Back when I was at middle school in the US, my dad would lie on his reclining sofa after dinner and practice his English with the TV on in the background. He'd look up words in his electronic dictionary and repeat them out loud.

One afternoon, my dad was dropping my friend Julia home after a sleepover. Out of nowhere, he asked, "Julia, how do you pronounce, uh, rabbit?"

Julia looked at me, bewildered, thinking she had misheard him. "Sorry, did you say rabbit?"

"Yes, rabbit," he said, looking at Julia in the rearview mirror. "R-r-r-rabbit. Can you understand me?"

I asked him to stop in Korean, but he continued to practice saying rabbit out loud, all the way to Julia's. I am still not sure if he was trying to embarrass me or was genuinely fixated on mastering his Rs, but I do now have a bit more sympathy for the social anxiety he must have felt. After all, it wasn't so dissimilar to what I'd experience growing up.

3

The Oxford year is divided into three eight-week terms; the rest is vacation, which meant I spent more than half my year in Norway during university, something, I am sure, that didn't slip my dad's mind as he paid the tuition fees. Apart from a few museums (I recommend the Munch, Fram and Kon-Tiki) and a vast sculpture park with a giant phallus as its centerpiece (which I also recommend), there wasn't a huge amount of sightseeing to do in Oslo. I tried to learn to cross-country ski, as my parents had—they once even made it into a local newspaper after enrolling in a ski competition—but I staggered and skidded as little Norwegian kids glided past me. To be fair, Norwegians are said to be born with skis on their feet.

And without any friends in Norway, my social life centered on the diplomatic schedule. Whenever I was visiting, I tagged along to the annual national day receptions hosted by each of the nearly seventy embassies in Oslo. It was always the same group of people from the diplomatic corps getting together reception after reception, so I was welcomed as a fresh face—there was only so much small talk one could manage.

Pretty much like in any other social gathering, there were hierarchies and cliques. Officially, the hierarchy was based on precedence—who had been in the post the longest—but there were other factors at play, like the strength of the country they were representing, their fluency in English and of course individual personalities, which could sometimes be quite different to what one might expect based on their countries' reputations, at least as portrayed in Western media. The Iraqi ambassador, for instance, was a lovely, bold woman, and the Saudi ambassador was the friendliest man who spoke perfect English.

Conversations often revolved around our record of postings, a strong bond created from having lived in the same country, and shared observations about life in Norway, mainly how expensive it is and how dark it gets in the winter. The ambassadors and spouses would ask me about my studies, then tell me how I reminded them of their own children. Except they had no idea what I was going through behind closed doors.

~

It would seem I had everything going for me: I was a student at Oxford and the daughter of the Korean ambassador. But all my many privileges couldn't stop me from thinking, *I want to die*. I've thought it through; I know what I'm doing. It's a rational decision. In fact, it's the only logical conclusion. I know I'll be happy again for a while if I stay alive, but soon enough I'll be depressed again. Happiness is fleeting; depression lasts and lasts and lasts.

I can't figure out what's wrong with me. I didn't have a traumatic childhood or abusive parents. There's no family history of mental illness. I even wonder if it has to do with some prenatal stress from being in my mother's womb during the war in Rwanda, but that seems far-fetched.

The only other suspect in my mind is the many international moves growing up, but I can't quite articulate how that would lead to my current depression. No, I should be feeling grateful—not resentful—that I had such a privileged global upbringing.

If I had real problems, there would at least be some hope. Once those problems were fixed, I might get better. But there's nothing objectively wrong in my life, which means there is no hope. I have everything going for me. As my mom would say, I can do anything I want in this world.

I spend all day wishing I could be dead. What's the point of it all anyway? We're all going to die. I know that if I don't do it now, I am only prolonging my misery and delaying the inevitable.

In April 2013, I have an "emergency consultation" organized by my mom through her Norwegian friend Berit, who is a doctor. Surrounded by a clinical psychologist, a psychiatrist and some medical students who all listen sympathetically, I try to articulate my feelings.

The report: *She describes symptoms that are consistent with depression, such as meaninglessness, hopelessness, lack of sleep and suicidal thoughts. Not considered at acute suicidal risk.* I am prescribed Cipralex for depression and Vallergan for sleep, neither of which I take.

My mom knows I'm depressed, and I know she desperately wants to help, but there is nothing she can do. She thinks my meaning-of-life issues would go away if I had a boyfriend. She doesn't mean to trivialize my depression. More than anything, she wants to believe that having a boyfriend will fix me.

If only it was that simple.

PART TWO

Uprooted

1991–2005

4

I don't have a first memory. In fact, my first-ish memories are from when I was five or six and living in Korea, and even those are hazy. But a lot had happened in my life by the age of five: I'd already mastered two international moves, to the US and back.

From what I can gather from photos, my family lived in a typical suburban American house with swings and a slide in the backyard, and a basketball hoop by the garage—there is a photo of me dribbling in our driveway. I have cornrows in this photo, apparently from a recent trip to Mexico.

I am riding a bike with training wheels in the cul-de-sac outside our house.

I am dressed up as Barney the purple dinosaur for my first Halloween.

I am on a helicopter in the Grand Canyon.

My signature pose is to raise one arm in a gesture that, in retrospect, looks worryingly like the Nazi salute. Apparently, I am trying to be the Statue of Liberty.

There is even a class photo of me. I'm seated in the middle row, wearing a pink Minnie Mouse shirt and denim skirt with shoulder straps, among a mix of white and Asian kids. A girl in the front row is holding up a sign that says "LINDGREN 1995." My mom says I called it Amber School after Amber the goat in the school farm.

She still asks me in disbelief, "Can you *really* not remember *any* of it?"

"No, I can't, and your asking doesn't help," I snap, mostly out of frustration with myself, that I can't recall a single thing: a teacher, a friend, a vacation, anything. I so wish I could—I can tell I was a happy child—but it's totally blank.

I have long suspected my childhood amnesia has been caused by the early relocations, my little brain shocked into erasing all prior memories—like a factory reset—to adapt, to cope, to survive. I don't tell my mom this. Having orchestrated no fewer than thirteen international moves, my mom would agree—rightly so—that moving is one of the most stressful life events. However, when it comes to children, the common refrain goes: "They'll be okay, they're only little." As if children are infinitely adaptable.

I recently read somewhere that plants can undergo something called "transplant shock" when they are uprooted and moved to a new environment. I thought, *Hah, plants don't even go to school!*

~

I started school a year early at the Korean age of seven. (In Korea, you are born aged one, then become a year older in the New Year by eating a traditional rice cake soup. Everyone born in the same calendar year is the same age. If you were born on December 31, you would turn two the next day. You can add *mahn* to specify your actual age. I started school at the Korean age of seven, or *mahn* five.)

The reason I started school early, besides a "head start" mentality running in the family—my mom, dad and brother all started school early too—was that my parents wanted me to have as much of a Korean education as possible before we moved overseas again. I was initially placed in a special class for a handful of students who had recently returned from abroad. My friend Moon-sun's dad had worked for Toyota in Japan, and I remember she had lots of Japanese stationery and Sailor Moon merchandise at her house. We lived in the same apartment block, so our moms carpooled, and she and I quarreled all the time about who got to sit in the middle seat. We once fought tooth and nail after I called her a "blockhead," a new word I'd picked up from a sitcom.

After a year, I joined the normal class in the main school building and became best friends with Sohee and Jongmoon. We called ourselves Charlie's Angels. I don't have too many memories from this time, but I can just remember the sports days and field trips and the games we used to play. We would practice jacks during recess and mount the climbing frame, oblivious to our underwear showing.

During PE and school assemblies, we stood in rows according to something called our "height number." I was number one, right at the front, if not number two. The boys loved to tease me and would call me shorty, short legs and peanut. I called one of them Octopus because his name sounded something like Octavian, but in Korean. Another boy in my class who was tall for his age would call me "little one," lift my skirt and run away. I, of course, chased him around and secretly liked it when adults told me he was only behaving that way because he fancied me.

At school, I learned to read and write *hangul*, which we were taught was one of the most scientific and logical alphabets in the world, invented from scratch by King Sejong the Great in 1446. I learned to sing our national anthem, and that our national flower is the hibiscus. I colored in the Korean flag as our teacher explained the symbolism: the red-and-blue yin and yang represent the positive and negative cosmic forces, while the black bars in the four corners represent the sky, earth, water and fire. Together, they symbolize the harmony of the universe, as well as the harmony and reunification of the Koreas.

I remember learning about the founding myth behind our deep 5,000-year history (which Koreans love to contrast with the trifling "500-year" history of America). As legend has it, a tiger and a bear prayed to Hwanung, the son of the Lord of Heaven, to be transformed into humans. Hwanung promised, "If you can each survive on twenty cloves of garlic and a bundle of mugwort and avoid sunlight for one hundred days, you'll become human." (It's unsurprising that garlic, which Koreans love and is said to have one hundred benefits and only one drawback—its potent smell—should feature so prominently in our founding myth.) The tiger gave up after twenty days and left the cave. The bear remained and was transformed into a woman. The bear-woman married Hwanung and gave birth to a son, Dangun, who founded the first kingdom of Korea, from which all Koreans are said to have descended. Dangun ruled for 1,500 years before becoming a mountain god.

It sounds harmless, not unlike Romulus and Remus being suckled by a she-wolf before founding the city of Rome and the Roman Kingdom, but I now realize that our founding myth is central to Korean ethnic nationalism, the idea that our nation is one race, one people, one *minjok*, a unified bloodline tracing all the way back to Dangun, our common prehistoric origin. This message is embedded right in the national curriculum, to be absorbed by children at school.

Each time we moved countries, I had to adapt to a new education system, but the most drastic differences in syllabus were, perhaps unsurprisingly, in history. When I was in middle school in America, for instance, I was learning about the Boston Tea Party, the Gettysburg Address and the Declaration of Independence. The important names to learn were George Washington, Abraham Lincoln and Alexander Hamilton. Then, when I returned to Korea at the age of fourteen, after six years abroad, I was back to learning Korean history.

I mean *Korean* history. The first few pages of each chapter of our textbook were reserved for world history in the corresponding period. But as soon as our teacher announced, "Class, this section will not be in scope for exams," you could hear big X's being drawn across those pages. If it wasn't going to be in the exams, there was no need to learn it.

In modern history, we learned how Japan annexed Korea in 1910, then deprived us of our freedom of the press, assembly and speech; how they tried to assimilate us, banning the teaching and speaking of Korean, and excluding Korean history from the curriculum; how they appropriated land from our farmers and sold it cheaply to their own; how they forced "comfort women" to become military prostitutes for the Imperial Japanese Army and conscripted millions of Koreans into forced labor.

We also learned about the brave and heroic independence movements of our forefathers: how in 1909, An Jung-geun assassinated Ito Hirobumi, the first Prime Minister of Japan, and was executed at the age of thirty; how thirty-three activists issued a Proclamation of Independence in 1919 and mass demonstrations spread across the country, lasting twelve months; how in 1932, Yun Bong-gil set off a bomb in Shanghai at a Japanese celebration in honor of Emperor Hirohito's birthday and was arrested at the scene to be executed at the age of twenty-four.

I don't doubt it's important to learn about our own history but in my experience, our lessons were taught to the exclusion of wider world history and in a way that reinforces anti-Japanese sentiment, which very much persists to this day. I know Koreans would protest that Japan has never formally apologized nor paid reparations for the comfort women. The territorial disputes on Dokdo, a group of islets on the East Sea (or the "Sea of Japan" as the Japanese call it), don't help.

Ethnic Koreans living in Japan have also long been discriminated against. The Japanese billionaire Masayoshi Son says he suffered verbal and physical abuse from his classmates for being Korean and contemplated taking his own life in school. Later, when he started his business ventures, he chose to go against the tide and revert to his ancestral Korean surname. Even though he is third generation, he is still called *Zainichi* in Japanese, a term implying temporary residence.

Sadly, I'm not sure Koreans are any more accepting. Korea is ethnically homogeneous, with immigrants making up less than 5 percent of the population today. Among the biggest group, the Chinese, there is a clear distinction between Chinese citizens of Korean descent (like our cleaner in Norway) and ethnic Chinese. The next biggest group is the migrant workers from Southeast Asia, mostly there to pick up the so-called 3D—dirty, dangerous and demeaning—jobs. Korea also began actively encouraging "marriage migration," recruiting "mail-order" brides, mainly from China, Vietnam and the Philippines, for rural and lower-class men who were unsuccessful in finding a partner domestically. Are these people treated any better than Koreans who emigrated to the US to establish dry cleaners, convenience stores and nail salons?

After three years in Korea, we moved to Paris when I was seventeen.

"What is history?" was written on the blackboard first day of class. No one wanted to be the first to answer except Elizabeth, a history buff hoping to read History at Oxford, like Mr. Bunch himself. She said something smart like, "It's the narrative written by the victorious blah blah."

When it was my turn, I muttered, "History is ... everything that's happened in the past?"

"Everything?" Mr. Bunch said, stroking his belly with his Grinch-like hands.

"Uh, maybe not everything." I already felt stupid. This

would never have happened in Korea. Not only would such a philosophical question ever be asked, but if it was, we would have been given a definition to memorize.

Our first essay topic was: "The Treaty of Versailles: Was it?" What did that even mean? I had never written a history essay, nor even heard of this treaty. I'd been too busy studying the Treaty of Ganghwa, signed in 1876. But I read the reading list and chronicled all the events that led up to it, starting from the assassination of Archduke Franz Ferdinand. It was a long essay.

For all my efforts, I got 11.5 out of 20. I'd never been graded out of 20, which was apparently the standard grading system in France, but I could do the math: 58 percent. What was the half-mark for? Mr. Bunch scrawled a series of comments in the margins: "Yes. But what are you trying to say?" How was I supposed to know? What *was* I trying to say? Mr. Bunch said history is not a regurgitation of facts; our essay should be an argument. It didn't make any sense. To me, history was memorizing dates and answering multiple-choice questions.

I was finally learning the bigger picture, the world history—the parts we crossed out with a big X in Korea. We learned about fascism and communism, the Spanish Civil War, the origins of the Cold War. Mr. Bunch would hand out contemporary cartoons, newspaper clips, encyclopedia articles and "different assessments of Stalin by historians." He recommended books like Frantz Fanon's *The Wretched of the Earth* and Arthur Koestler's *Darkness at Noon* and urged us to read Solzhenitsyn.

In Korea, I had studied in close detail the thirty-five

years of brutal Japanese occupation. I'd learned about the tireless resistance movements, which ultimately led to our independence on August 15, 1945. It turned out, from another historical perspective, our liberation could be summed up in one sentence: "Following the victory of the Allies in 1945, Japan gave up its colonies, including Korea." So much for the heroic efforts of my forefathers, Korea was an afterthought.

I still have an article on the Korean War that Mr. Bunch handed out to us. It is photocopied from the *Modern History Review*. It says: "Korea played practically no role in the high diplomatic stakes of the great imperial powers." South Korea is referred to as "a land that very few Americans could even find on a map." History is all about perspective.

Mr. Bunch was, of course, a product of his own education and upbringing. He made a point of pronouncing pre-independence Kenya as "Keenya"—the British colonial way—and often spoke of "our colonies" with what sounded like nostalgia.

Perhaps the most important lesson I learned is that we are *all* a product of our education and upbringing, and that you can't take for granted what they teach you at school.

5

My mom says every pain of labor vanished when the nurse exclaimed, "It's a girl!" She had been expecting another boy based on the ultrasound scans she had done furtively (prenatal sex screening was illegal in Korea at the time due to selective female abortions being commonplace). My mom, however, had desperately hoped for a daughter. So, even at a full 4.0 kilos—I was ten days overdue—I was a nice surprise.

Typically in Confucian cultures, sons—the eldest son in particular—secure the lion's share of love in the family. That should have been my brother, who was the firstborn grandchild on my mom's side. But my brother was born in Portugal during my dad's first-ever posting and spent his early days there and then in Rwanda. Whereas I was born not only in Korea but at my grandpa's hospital, where he was an orthopedic surgeon. In between patients, he was dropping in and out of the delivery room—"any news yet?"—and rushed in to dote as soon as I was born. Despite being a traditional, patriarchal man, my grandpa was smitten, and I—a girl— stole my brother's limelight.

I don't know if this explains why my brother and I

never got along as far as I can remember. In early photos from America, he seems to be looking at me with love and affection. We are holding hands, or he has his arm wrapped around my shoulder unless he is being goofy and doing the bunny ears behind my back as I stand on tippy toes to look taller next to him.

My brother was one mischievous boy. Once, my Gunsan halmoni came to stay with us in America and on her last day, she asked my brother, who must have been eight then, how to ask for the toilet in English. Unsuspecting, she went around JFK repeating, "Grandma eats poo." You can imagine the kind of pranks he pulled on his younger sister.

But it was more than that. He liked to bully me, not in a playful older sibling way, but with a visceral hatred. My parents would tell us to care for each other because we were each other's "one and only sibling." I hated that. I'm sure he hated it as much as I did. I yearned for the protective older brother who beat up the mean kids at school and said things like, "Don't mess with my sister." Not a brother who beat me up himself.

I'm not allowed to call my brother by his name. I have to call him *oppa*, which is the Korean term for older brother when spoken by a girl. My brother, on the other hand, can call me by my name since he is older, though he called me anything but. One that really wound me up was "Bokneh," some random hillbilly character from his Korean literature text.

"Umma, he's calling me Bokneh again. Tell him to stop," I'd whine.

"Seung Gon, stop calling your sister Bokneh."

40

"Okay, RWEE-nah," he'd come back with a smirk.

I would try to get even by calling him by his name, "Ya! Seung Gon," but that never ended well for me.

Funnily enough, it's thanks to my brother I was named Lena.

My brother was named Soo Hyuk at birth. But he was born in Lisbon, where the best the Portuguese could enunciate was Soo Yuck. To avoid their son being called "yuck," my parents started calling my brother Um, which means "one" in Portuguese. He was their number one. And it ensured the Portuguese could pronounce his name.

But my grandfather—my dad's dad, who died before I was born—wasn't impressed with Um. Even though Soo Hyuk had been his idea, he now insisted my brother's name should end with Gon, which was the *dolimja* or generational syllable in our family. (Korean first names are usually two syllables, and one of them is often shared among siblings and cousins. For instance, my mom's siblings are called Kee Ho, Kee Won and Kee Jung.)

Despite my mom's meek protests, my grandfather wanted to call my brother Uhn Gon and had his name legally changed. This would have required a court application, but my grandfather was a local government official and sorted this one out with a handshake.

The naming fiasco wasn't over for my brother. By this time, my dad was posted to Rwanda and now the Rwandans couldn't pronounce Uhn Gon. Also, it was ugly. So, when her father-in-law died, my mom changed my brother's legal name again to Seung Gon, keeping the Gon syllable out of respect.

By the time I came around, my parents sought the help of a traditional namer, whose job it was to work out astrologically auspicious names for the date and time of my birth. My parents didn't believe in that kind of stuff; they just asked for a name that anyone in the world could pronounce. It took so long to find one, they had to pay a late fine for my birth registration, but it was worth the wait.

Nowadays, some people will ask me, "What's your *real* name? Like your Korean name."

"Lena *is* my real name," I say defiantly.

6

There is a great family photo from my *dol* or first birthday. My mom is dressed elegantly in a hot-pink suit with a chiffon scarf wrapped around her neck; my dad is in a suit and tie; and my brother, only five, is sitting on my grandpa's lap. My grandma, in an oversized red blouse with a pearl brooch pinned at the top, looks startlingly young. I am wrapped up in a bright green-and-yellow hanbok, with an even more colorful collar and cuffs, topped off with a gold-embossed hat with little earflaps.

We are all sitting on the floor behind a low table laid out with plates of fruits: mounds of apples, oranges, kiwis, strawberries, *chamoe*—a Korean melon that has a thin, yellow edible skin and white streaks running along the rind—and a big bunch of bananas. There are all different kinds of rice cakes stacked high to symbolize prosperity, the tradition dating back to a time when many infants didn't make it past their first birthday.

The highlight of the ceremony is a fortune-telling custom where various objects are placed in front of the child, and they are urged to pick one up. Grabbing money or grain

43

augured wealth; the noodle or thread foretold longevity; the bow or arrow signified title and rank.

Looking clueless with my enormous cheeks, I grabbed the pen.

Maybe I was destined to write?

~

A fortune teller once told my grandpa—my mom's dad—that he would live to sixty if he made it to forty, but it was unlikely he would make it to forty. Somewhat superstitious, my grandma had to do something for fear that he really would die before forty. So, a piglet was delivered from the countryside in an ambulance borrowed from my grandpa's hospital and placed in the family bathtub in Seoul. Before each meal, the piglet was fed rice with a silver spoon. Then, after one hundred days of being literally spoon-fed, the piglet was taken back to the countryside to be sacrificed. My mom, who was ten at the time, says she was mortified by the constant oinking when her friends came around. But in the end, my grandpa did make it past forty, and sixty too (though not by much longer).

My grandpa looked like a Korean Al Pacino, a larger-than-life figure with deep-set eyes, thick eyebrows, thick lips and thick black hair, despite a receding hairline. When I kissed his cheeks, his stubble grated on my skin and his breath stank of tobacco and alcohol. But I loved him a lot, partly because he showered me with presents that my mom didn't approve of, once an animal crystal figurine which I dropped on the floor just as I was opening it ("I told you she's too young for this!"). He doted on me and would spank my brother when he'd had enough. I was very much the favorite.

My grandma lived in his shadows, catering to her husband's needs, until his death. She carries in her bones what Koreans call *han*—a deep sorrow, grief, anger—and continually laments her *palja*—fate. Born the first of eight children in 1936 when Korea was still under Japanese occupation, my grandma practically raised her siblings, feeding them first when there wasn't enough food to go around. Then, when she was a young teen, her family fled to Daegu, where her father was a military doctor during the Korean War. After the armistice, they moved to Seoul, and she went on to study pharmacy at Ewha, the same prestigious university my mom would go to.

But my grandpa would not let his wife work—or drive—and her skills were best exhibited in the kitchen. My grandpa was a gourmet who needed all his meals cooked properly, including a pot of scorched rice nurungji soup at the end. Luckily for him, my grandma was (and is) a wonderful cook, all her dishes infused with her *son-mat*, literally "hand taste," a certain Korean *je ne sais quoi*. My favorite was her famously tender galbijjim or braised beef short ribs, a highly time- and labor-intensive dish that she was happy to make for us.

Thanks to my grandpa regularly convening family meals, I saw my mom's side often when I lived in Korea. They felt warm, soft and fuzzy to me, just like my mom. But Korea being a patrilineal society, it was my dad's side I saw for traditional holidays. It always felt stilted with them. It may have been because I only saw them a few times a year, but I don't think the five siblings got on well, someone or other not talking to each other at any given time. While I spoke to all my aunts and uncles on my mom's side in the informal form, I used the honorific form with my dad's side. (I also have little memory of my dad from this time. It coincided with the Asian financial crisis—which Koreans refer to as the "IMF crisis" even though it was the International Monetary Fund which bailed us out in 1997—so I think he often worked late and came home after I went to bed.)

During *seollal*, or the Lunar New Year, the kids took turns bowing deeply to the adults, starting with my Gunsan halmoni. Dressed in my hanbok, I would clasp my right hand on top, as prescribed for girls (it was the opposite hand for boys) and bring them to my head as I kneeled and kissed my forehead to the floor. "I wish you lots of good fortune in the new year," I'd say in my best voice. Then my grandmother would hand me an envelope, which I'd receive respectfully with both hands. As soon as the bowing merry-go-round was over, the children scurried away to count their cash.

"How much did you get?" my brother would ask. He usually got more money than me, which I wasn't happy about but accepted as he was older. What really upset me was when I found out my cousin Minhee, who was a year younger than me and had to call me *noona*, the way I had to call my brother *oppa*, received more money than me because he was a boy. That was my Gunsan halmoni.

The main holiday growing up was *chuseok*, or the "Korean Thanksgiving," a harvest festival in the autumn. It wasn't much of a holiday, though, for my mom. As the eldest son's wife, she was responsible for preparing the feast to honor our dead ancestors, or really, to appease her in-laws. Her position in the family was made clear by a highly elaborate system of kinship terms. For instance, *doryunnim* is the term she used to address her brother-in-law-who-is-younger-than-her-husband-and-unmarried, but not when speaking of him, for which there was another term. His title would also change if he married. I still find the terminology hugely confusing—it's never just "aunts" and "uncles"—but distinguishing whose side of the family someone is on and whether they are related by blood or marriage is an important aspect of Korean culture.

The food would be stacked high on silver plates which looked like footed cake stands and had to be laid out in a specific order on a special low, lacquered table. As I shuttled back and forth from the kitchen balancing the plates, my dad would check his little handbook before telling me what went where. Fruits—apples, pears (the Korean kind which are round and hard), persimmons, chestnuts, dried dates—went on the closest edge of the table. Red fruits went to the east; white fruits to the west. With big fruits like apples and pears, we were only to place an odd number of them, and we'd slice off a bit to make them accessible for our ancestors. The next rows were filled with Korean pancakes, seasoned vegetables, meats and fish—the head facing east. The final row was for steamed rice and soup. An ancestral tablet was placed in the deepest part of the table and a candle laid on each end. We also put a photograph of my dad's dad in his police uniform.

For the ceremony, my dad, brother, uncles and two male

47

cousins stood in the front row, while I stood in the back with my mom, aunts and two female cousins. My dad would recite some incomprehensible ritual greeting from the handbook in a funny voice, like a pastor at a church, then make the first offering of rice wine. He would kneel before the altar and rotate the cup three times counterclockwise over some incense before dumping the wine into an empty bowl in three goes.

The kids waited to be called upon. "What do you think your grandfather would like to eat next?" my dad would ask. When it was my turn, I picked up the chopsticks, tapped the ends on the table to align them (always twice), then placed them on whatever dish I wanted to eat. After my dad served the main course by sticking a spoon into the rice bowl, we'd wait in silence for a few minutes. The mood was always somber, or at least solemn, to be respectful of our dead ancestors who were savoring their meals. Then we bowed down to our knees and kissed our foreheads to the floor. The men and boys only had to do two bows, whereas the women and girls had to do four. I would peer at my mom to make sure I was bowing in sync with everyone else.

After the cumbersome ritual, we'd sit around the low table and feast. When my Gunsan halmoni declared she was finished with her meal, it was imperative to insist, "Halmoni, please have some more. You've barely eaten!" Even when she waved her hands and said she'd had enough, it was wise to insist until she gave in—she always did. The washing up was, of course, my mom's responsibility.

As part of the holiday, we also visited our ancestors' graves in the countryside, though for some reason I only ever remember doing this with my mom's family. Everyone would pile into a few cars and set off early to avoid the traffic. At rest stops, we'd get corn dogs and dried squid, which would be ripped apart and distributed according to individual preferences (there are said to be two kinds of Korean people: those who like the crispy legs and those who like the chewy body). When we arrived at the site, we would set up a picnic mat in front of the burial mounds where my great-grandparents were laid to rest and do a quick ceremony involving some more bowing. The adults would spray soju on the mounds and remove the weeds around the epitaphs before we joined the highway traffic back to Seoul.

7

On my last day of school in Korea, in the middle of third grade, my teacher gave me a big baby blue album. On the first page was a letter he'd typed up for me, which must have been a technologically advanced thing to do in those days. He reassured me that even though I'd be sad to say goodbye to my friends, I'd make new ones easily. He reminded me to "always be grateful to your admirable parents who have given you this opportunity to see and experience the wider world."

The rest of the album was filled with more letters. Unbeknown to me, my teacher must have briefed the class that their classmate Lena was moving to this hot and humid country called Malaysia for her father's job. Would they write her a message and bring a photo for her to remember them by? The letters are written on all kinds of Korean stationery, in colorful pens and even more colorful penmanship. Some look like an edited manuscript, with words crossed out and inserted with arrows. Some enclosed passport photos, others holiday snapshots.

Most of my classmates must have forgotten the name of this elusive country by the time they got home. Malaysia

50

is variously referred to as Nigeria, "Ma-leh-ya-ji" and "Malehnesia or whatever that country is called." One friend avoids any reference to Malaysia: "I'm sad to hear you are moving to a hot country." Another wonders, "How are you going to cope in such a hot country as Malaysia? Here's what I think. Korea isn't as hot as Malaysia—how agonizing to make that even hotter." One must have missed the message entirely and gifted me a set of white furry earmuffs.

"But you can't even speak English," one girl worries for me, while another tells me not to forget Korean. I am reminded to go to school in Malaysia.

One boy says, "Can I come with you? I wish I could go anywhere abroad. You're lucky. Pff, I'm sure I could go with my family too. Except I wish I could go now."

A few boys confess their love: "This is a secret, but I fell in love with you in second grade. It would be too bad if you didn't like me back." What can I say?

Friends wrote down their home addresses, promising to keep in touch, asking me to remember them by their photos. They'll wait for me to send them mine.

∽

The flight to Malaysia is the first that I can remember, and I loved it so much I decided that I wanted to become a "stew-uh-dess" when I grew up. The ladies were so lovely and smiley and kept bringing me peanuts and juices. I imagined myself in a Korean Air uniform one day. I also clearly remember asking my mom on the flight if we were going to become Malaysian once we landed in Malaysia. "No, honey, we'll still be Koreans," she said with a chuckle.

Seven hours later, we arrived at the shiny, newly built international airport in Kuala Lumpur where the local women seemed to float around, draped head to toe in black. I wondered how they saw where they were going. After we stacked our luggage high on trolleys, my mom told me and my brother to keep quiet as we passed through security. She explained that dogs were considered unclean and impure here, and that the locals may not like Jjanga, who was hidden inside a plastic kennel at the bottom of a trolley. I held my breath and Jjanga didn't bark either. She was successfully smuggled into the country.

My brother and I both enrolled at the international school, a sprawling open-air campus with palm trees, a big pool and grass fields, though the elementary and middle schools were sufficiently separated that we rarely bumped into each other. Even when we did, we looked straight past each other the way a cow looks at a chicken, to use a Korean idiom. There were plenty of other Koreans and Lees at the school, so I don't think anyone knew we were siblings.

I don't remember my first day of school, but I am still grateful to my friend June Kyoung, or June as she was called by foreigners. I would constantly tap her and ask in Korean, "What's the teacher saying?" When we first arrived in Malaysia, I couldn't speak any English—I remember getting "chicken" and "kitchen" confused—even though I'd been speaking it fluently three years earlier.

My mom tells me that I didn't speak a word of English during my first year at Amber School, the nursery in America. She was reassured by my teacher, though, that even though

I wasn't speaking, she was sure I understood what she was saying. And because I was speaking Korean at home, my mom knew I wasn't mute. Then, a year later, I started speaking in English fluently. But then after spending three years in Korea, it seemed my knowledge of the language had evaporated.

June interpreted patiently for me, without once wincing or shushing me so she could at least hear the instructions. My teacher noted in my first semester report that I was "a little shy and doesn't readily speak in English." By the second semester though: "She is conversing in English very well and no longer relies on others to translate for her." I was lucky to have someone like June help me, and I took intensive English as a Second Language (ESL) classes the first year, but I must have been aided by my unconscious memory of the English language, sitting latent somewhere in my brain, ready to be reactivated like muscle memory.

June was calm and mature beyond her age. She showed me around the vast campus until I could find my way and taught me lots of other things like the fact that teachers were called "Mr." and "Mrs." and not "Teacher" as we'd called them in Korea. She wore these round, silver-rimmed glasses, and I wanted a pair just like hers. I probably would have needed them anyway thanks to my dad's genes, but I may have expedited the process by reading my piano notes in the dark on purpose. For my first pair, I chose the same round glasses with shiny silver rims, but June was the kind of person who didn't even mind me copying her.

Within a year, I blossomed from the quiet girl who needed an interpreter to a lively and confident one who liked to socialize (excessively) during class.

One of the best things about Malaysia was the cuisine, a most exquisite blend of Chinese, Malay and Indian flavors mirroring the country's multiethnic heritage. It had the best of each world, but its own unique take on it too. There were sizzling woks, dim sum, satay, steamboats, tom yum, nasi goreng and wonton soup to name a few of our favorite dishes.

The best food was always found in the humblest joints, where chefs tossed noodles in the air and stirred gigantic cast-iron woks engulfed by fire. For seafood, my family frequented a run-down Chinese restaurant where we'd order so much food, we had to finish plates to make space for more. It was pure joy feasting on these dishes as dusty old ceiling fans whirred above us. Nowadays, when I see "king prawns" in Western supermarkets, I think back to what real prawns looked like in Malaysia.

The roti canai would be fried to perfection and served crispy golden on a steel tray. My mom and I would tear the piping hot doughy bread with our fingers and dip it into different flavors of curries before savoring each bite. For banmian, we were loyal to this one Chinese lady who ran a tiny booth with a few red plastic tables and chairs. There was only one dish, so we didn't even need to look at the menu. Minutes later, we'd be slurping the hearty soup with fresh handmade noodles, mushrooms and leafy green vegetables. The ingredients may have been modest, but the food was magical.

I tried so many delicious foods for the first time, including lamb chops. My mom didn't like the distinctive smell as Koreans traditionally don't eat lamb, but she always encouraged me and my brother to try new foods. We loved it.

Oh, and the fruits! There were so many sweet, succulent tropical fruits we'd never had before, like rambutan, soursop, jackfruit and pomelo. After dinner, my family would sit in the living room and dig into a huge tray of mangosteen, sucking on the white juicy bits and leaving a mountain of mangosteen carcass.

Some evenings after dinner we drove to our durian place, a roadside stall, where the vendor would skillfully wedge open the spiky fruit into two hemispheres of a brain. The insides were a gooey yellow and gave off a pungent gassy smell, but we learned to love the strange creamy taste, the texture of a meaty avocado, but stringy like a ripe mango.

It was wonderful.

8

"Grandpa died," my brother said, looking straight into my mom's eyes, emotionless, as if he was stating any other mundane fact. It was the last day of our family cruise around Southeast Asia the summer I graduated from elementary school and my brother from middle school. We'd gone snorkeling in Langkawi and shopping in Phuket. I skipped up and down the corridors of the titanic ship. We were having so much fun my brother and I barely fought.

My mom froze at the entrance to our cabin, water still dripping from her hair. She and I had been swimming on the top deck for the last time before we had to pack up our bags. "Seung Gon," she said, "you should never joke about things like that." Her eyes were scolding him as if to say, "I taught you better than that," but her voice was already quivering.

My brother held her gaze silently, causing my mom to well up and collapse onto the bunk bed. My dad burst in soon after. "Where have you been? I've been looking all over for you."

At ten years old, I knew people died, but I didn't really understand what it meant, how final death was. Not long before, my grandparents had come to visit us in Malaysia, and we all went to Tioman Island together. I snorkeled for the first time on the most beautiful, pristine beaches and we saw clunky Komodo dragons roaming around like warriors. One day my grandpa went fishing with the local men—he didn't allow women near the boat—and we started to worry when he didn't come back late into the afternoon. "He's either having a bonanza or still hasn't caught one fish," my grandma said, based on many years of experience. We were so relieved when he came back grinning with bucket loads of fish, which we cooked for dinner that evening. And now he was gone?

It was most unexpected. As the former president of the Korean Medical Association, my grandpa had been on a foreign aid visit to North Korea when he passed away. We were told he had been found unconscious in the hotel bathroom the morning after he arrived in Pyongyang. He was transferred to the local emergency room, but it was too late. His death was reported on the news, the first civilian body to be carried directly across the demilitarized zone (rather than flown via Beijing), as negotiated by the Ministry of Unification. My uncles received his body from the North Korean government at the Joint Security Area of Panmunjom.

They said it was a brain hemorrhage. My grandpa was a big smoker and drinker, and he did have some underlying health conditions, but it felt sinister that he had died in North Korea of all places. I wondered if there had been foul play. Or at least if he would have made it had he been treated in South Korea.

My family was escorted off the cruise before any of the other passengers disembarked, and we took the first flight back to Korea. We were taken straight to a building within hospital grounds where the funeral was held. I had never been to a funeral and didn't know what to expect. There was an electronic display at the entrance, like the arrivals and departures board at airports but showing the names of the deceased and the room number instead of the gate. Other mourners dressed in black were loitering in the lobby, taking a cigarette break or getting a breath of fresh air. My body still felt like it was rocking from being at sea.

The walls outside my grandpa's mourning room were lined with huge floral arrangements, each with two long white sashes. All my extended family was inside, standing shoulder to shoulder. My aunt came to hug me as soon as she saw me, though I couldn't tell if she was crying because her father had died or smiling because she was happy to see me. "He loved you so much, Lena," she said. Everyone's eyes were pink and puffy and looked half-closed from sleep deprivation. It was upsetting to see my family, especially my mom, weep. I'd never seen her look so fragile and broken. Now that I am older and living on the other side of the world to my parents, I can imagine what it must have felt like for her: the shock, the disbelief, the guilt. She didn't even have a chance to say goodbye. Her father was now a portrait in the middle of an altar full of white chrysanthemums, two black ribbons hung around the corners of the frame.

Funerals are typically three-day events in Korea, but my grandpa's was extended to five days to accommodate my family's late arrival from Malaysia. As the eldest son, my mom's younger brother was the *sangju*, or the chief mourner responsible for organizing the funeral. Over his black suit, he wore two white stripes on his left arm, like armbands worn by a soccer captain.

Guests streamed in to give their condolences. There were many older people, my grandpa's friends and colleagues, and I recognized some of my mom's many friends. One of my roles was to hand out a chrysanthemum after they had signed the guest book and given us an envelope with condolence money. The guests bowed to my grandpa's photo in the mourning room, then placed the chrysanthemum on the altar. After paying their respects, they moved into the vast dining hall, which was run like a restaurant by our family. I hopped from table to table asking if anyone would like more soju or beer. When they left, I threw away the empty paper plates and replenished the table with more dried snacks and side dishes. My mom sometimes sat with her friends, and I could tell she was swallowing her tears. At times, the mood in the dining room felt too boisterous, almost festive. I complained to my mom when they burst into laughter, but she told me we should be grateful they were keeping the place alive.

On the last day of mourning, the adults from our immediate family went to see my grandpa. As the favorite grandchild, I was allowed to follow them. Through a big rectangular window, we saw his body stretched out on a gurney, covered in a white cloth. My mom and her siblings went in to see him up close. I sobbed, watching his children stroke him one last time. It was my first time seeing a dead body and I couldn't believe that was my grandpa. If I hadn't understood death before, it was clear to me then.

The fifth day was his burial. It was a rainy day. The men

in the family carried the casket and led the procession to the hearse. We drove a few hours south to his hometown where the burial mounds were, where we used to go during chuseok. It had always seemed like a place for long-gone ancestors. We huddled under umbrellas and watched solemnly as the ground was dug and the casket lowered. An elderly gentleman, a friend of my grandpa's it must have been, nudged my brother and said, "You must be the grandchild he loved so dearly. How he spoke of you!"

My brother shook his head and pointed at me. "No, that's her."

~

After spending the summer in Korea, I entered middle school for my third and final year in Malaysia. A few weeks after school started, my mom woke me up one night. "You have to come see this," she said, panic in her voice. I followed her to the living room, where my dad was transfixed in front of the TV. On the screen thick plumes of smoke billowed as two skyscrapers collapsed to the ground. Except for the knowledge that the world had changed forever, no one knew how to process this.

Both my mind and body were growing but not at the same speeds, frustratingly. At school, some girls were now a head taller than me and growing curves. I was not only a year or two younger but small for my age, resulting in a growing mismatch between the way I looked on the outside and how I felt inside. I didn't want to be the little girl with the lace ruffle socks and cartoons on my underwear. If only I could will my body to grow taller and my boobs to grow bigger.

As I was now in middle school, there was a school dance night. I wanted to look sexy and sophisticated for the occasion, not like the ten-year-old that I was. The children's stores only had fairy princess dresses with puff sleeves and giant ribbons, so my mom took me shopping to the adult section, which had elegant dresses with plunging necklines, but even the size 0 was too big for me. In the end, my mom custom-made a dress for me. She bought some black fabric with frills, cut it to my size and attached silver beads as shoulder straps. Hair and makeup done, I borrowed her jewelry and wore one-inch heels. Looking back through photos, I am taken aback by how young I look. I remember feeling so much older.

~

When we first moved to Malaysia, my parents struggled to get used to the year-round equatorial heat, whereas I had no trouble acclimatizing. In fact, I practically over-adapted as I needed a jacket to keep me warm when I returned to Korea during the summer. But I remember it being unbearably hot one day when I came home from school. My room felt like a furnace, the sun blasting through the windows. The heat made me angry. Suddenly, out of nowhere, I decided I didn't want to live anymore. I stepped on a stool, opened the window and stuck my head out. Immediately, my head started spinning. We were on the fifteenth floor. The ground was far away, a lot farther than I'd expected. Overcome with vertigo, I came off the stool and closed the window.

I didn't think much of this incident until years later when I was reading Albert Camus's *L'Étranger* at my French high school. I identified my younger self with Meursault, the protagonist who kills an Arab man on the beach for no apparent reason other than the oppressive heat of the sun. There was no premeditation on my part either. It was the heat of the moment. I wasn't depressed, nor was this a suicide attempt, but it reflects some perverse suicidal urge, at age ten, ostensibly because it was too hot.

There's also something I wrote around this time: *Just like I read in the book, life is an earthly version of hell, because it sucks like it. I'd like to suicide. P.S. Hope my math test goes OK or even better.* I have no idea which book I'd read. Ironically, this is written in a bubblegum pink diary that says "happy songs of memory" on the cover, with a quote (in English) typical of Korean stationery: "Forty years after, this diary will soothe your loneliness and boredom, like an old pop song."

Whatever it was I was going through, I started taking it out on my mom. One day, when a friend was over at my house, I started screaming at my mom, like I'd never screamed before, tears streaming down my face. I don't remember why, but she was yelling at me too. I must have screamed myself to sleep because I only remember waking up hours later. My friend had gone home. I didn't speak to my mom, not a single word, for three months. Eventually, my dad staged an intervention and wrote a letter to my mom in my handwriting, saying I was sorry. I reluctantly agreed that he could give it to her, and we made up. But this was a turning point in our relationship. My mom remembers it as the violent onset of what would be a prolonged period of turbulent adolescence.

The angelic days, as she described them, were over.

9

There is a Confucian saying that Mencius's mother moved three times before she found a suitable location to raise her son. And that is how Mencius became the great Chinese philosopher, the "second sage" of Confucianism. It was with the same noble intention that my family ended up in Franklin Lakes, New Jersey, when we moved to the US in the summer of 2002.

After three years in Malaysia, my dad was posted to the United Nations for a second time. As my brother and I would be attending the local public school, location was crucial. During our first stint in the US, we had lived in Cresskill, on the eastern border of Bergen County. This area would have been convenient for my dad to commute into Manhattan, and there were many nice suburbs with highly rated public schools, but that was also the problem: it attracted too many Koreans. There was a large Koreatown in Fort Lee, with signs in *hangul* as common as in English. (Fort Lee is named after General Charles Lee who served in George Washington's time but may as well have been named after all the Korean Lees living in the area.) My parents didn't

64

want us settling into a Korean enclave in the US, making Korean friends and speaking in Korean, as my brother had done in Malaysia. They felt even more pressure to get it right as my brother was now in high school. Having scoured all of Bergen County, we ended up in Franklin Lakes, a mere 50 kilometers (or 30 miles) each way for my dad. With traffic on the George Washington Bridge and the Manhattan gridlock, his commute could easily consume three hours of his day, all to ensure a good school, a good environment for me and my brother.

Franklin Lakes was a town of ten thousand people, and I went to the one middle school in the borough. I had finished sixth grade in Malaysia, but my parents thought I could benefit from being in the right age group, so I re-enrolled in the sixth grade. Plus, this way, by joining at the start of middle school, I wouldn't have to stand out as the new girl.

Thankfully, I wasn't "fresh off the boat." Coming from Malaysia, I was fluent in English and had been exposed to a Western education. But what immediately struck me on my first day of school was the whiteness. Of 170 students in my year, a dozen were East Asian, a dozen were South Asian, and only two were black, one girl and one boy. Everyone else was white.

When I was in Malaysia, I had friends from all over the world, from Argentina and Sweden to Namibia and Kuwait, like a mini-UN, though with significant overrepresentation from the US and Korea. We celebrated cultural diversity at every opportunity. There'd be flag parades, food stalls and traditional dance and music performances for the school's annual international festival. Students, parents and teachers alike donned their national costumes: kimonos, kilts, hanbok, sombreros. My mom loved to dress me up: in a moss green sari with sparkly beads for Deepavali, the Hindu festival of lights; a loose, knee-length purple dress over a long skirt for Hari Raya, which is celebrated by the local Muslim community.

My new school was not only predominantly white but overwhelmingly American. At my international school, the white kids had hailed from all over the world—France, Finland, Australia and also America. Here, almost everyone was American. Judging by their family names, many were probably of Italian and Irish origin—there was also a big Jewish community, with many bar and bat mitzvahs to come—though we never discussed things like ancestry back then.

I knew that if I did nothing, I'd be marked for the Asian group. Even in Malaysia, ethnic groups tended to stick together. My brother, for instance, was in the Korean group. Even though he spoke English fluently, all his friends were Korean. He followed Korean fashion trends, like bleaching and spiking the front of his hair. I, on the other hand, had some Korean friends, including June, but also friends who were Malaysian, white American, black American. One of my best friends, Melissa, was half-American and half-Korean.

The Asians at my new school were mostly Asian-American, though a few had heavy accents and couldn't distinguish between "sheet" and "shit." They also had funny names, one of the many reasons I dreaded first days of school. Yes, here, present, until the inevitable, "Oh, I am so sorry, I'm going to mispronounce this one. Is it Nahhh-uh-kyo-anggg?" Everyone would look around until a meek

Asian girl put her hand up. I thanked God that was not me.

I didn't want to be the Asian nerd who kids only spoke to for homework, the classmate no one recognized in the yearbook. That was not me. I refused to be reduced to a stereotype.

~

I met Mary on the school orientation trip and Julia through a partner project, and we became BFFs in no time, the way kids do. At school, we had different classes, but we had lunch together in the canteen and hung out at recess. After school, we'd go to the local pizza parlor or arrange for our parents to take us to the mall or the movies. We went over to each other's houses as if they were our second homes.

There were the strictest rules at Mary's house—Mary had three older brothers, Joe, Tom and Mike, and her parents were protective of their youngest—but we also had the most fun there. They had a big pool where we would do handstands and play Marco Polo and cannonball and belly flop off the diving board. Her middle brother, Tom, would take us quad biking in the woods behind her house, and it was exhilarating zooming up in the air and landing with a bump.

Mary also had a trampoline where we would practice doing the splits for the cheerleading squad and just be silly without a care in the world. One day at school we learned about bird regurgitation and found this so fascinating that we decided to try it ourselves. I was the mother bird and Mary was the chick. I gulped some Gatorade and tried to direct a stream to Mary, who was lying on the trampoline with her mouth wide open, ready to be fed. We started laughing so much I spewed the Gatorade all over her. It was hilarious—you had to be there.

One of our favorite pastimes was ding dong ditching. For camouflage but mostly for fun, we'd all dress in black and smear dark eyeshadow on our faces before heading out in the evening. We would ring the neighbors' doorbells and run away to hide in the bushes or sometimes right behind their door column, trying not to laugh as we watched them come out and look around suspiciously. The best part was to ring a second and third time until they shouted, "I'm going to call the police!" We took care to rotate the neighborhoods.

We also loved watching horror movies like *The Blair Witch Project* and *FeardotCom* (still rented from Blockbuster). Once, after watching *The Ring*, Julia and I were getting some late-night snacks from the kitchen when her house phone rang. It was past midnight. We looked at each other, petrified, then sprinted up the stairs to wake up her parents. It turned out Julia's older sister overheard us watching the movie from her room next door and thought it would be a funny prank. Her parents were not pleased. Julia and I thought we were dying, really. It gave us the idea to do likewise though, and we made prank calls to kids at our school, whispering "seven days" in a raspy voice before promptly hanging up.

One July day, after an afternoon of trampolining—Mary's trampoline seems to be a place of many memories for me—I saw a drop of blood on my underwear. At first, I thought it was because someone had accidentally kicked me when we were jumping around, but of course it was my period. I was the first of my friends. We Asked Jeeves "how to insert a tampon" and "do you lose your virginity if you use a tampon?" After failing to insert one, I borrowed a pad from Mary's mom. It felt like a diaper.

10

I fell in love with Limited Too the first time I went shopping in America before the start of school and wished the entire store could be my wardrobe. After a rigorous selection process, my mom let me buy a pair of flared jeans, which had a light wash on the thighs, shiny studs down the sides and glitter at the bottom. They came with a grommet belt that looked too cool. It would be perfect for my first day.

Unfortunately, the girls at my school were ridiculously sophisticated and didn't wear kids' brands like Limited Too. They sported designer handbags—Fendi, Dior, Gucci, Louis Vuitton, Prada—to school. I felt tacky wearing my red Eastpak, which my mom had newly bought me. It was the first time I got to choose my outfit to school—I'd worn uniforms in Korea and Malaysia—and I became obsessed with fashion, which turned into a major source of friction with my mom, most trips to the mall ending in me throwing a tantrum and a silent drive home.

"You never buy me anything!"

"Just wait a few weeks. It'll be on sale."

In my eleven-year-old eyes, my mom just didn't get it. I wrote: *Jan 23, 2003. Mom's so annoying. "Do math! Do* math!" 'n she thinks I don't study?! Go ask any of my friends. Ur lucky to have me. With mom, her life is based on grades. With me, it's based on social life and fashion. I really don't get along with her.

Here's another one from just two days later: *Dear Diary, my life is a serious living hell. It's too complicated. I hate my mom forever. She's so out of fashion. She's obsessed with Gap. Jeez!*

My mom's favorite stores were Gap and Old Navy, which had year-round sales on but were emphatically not your ticket to middle school social acceptance. My brother was less interested in fashion and more open to wearing my mom's bargain purchases, though when she bought him a navy zip hoodie with "OLD NAVY" stitched in giant white letters, that was too much even for him. "Look, it's perfectly good quality," my mom said, after unstitching each letter.

It was better for both me and my mom if I went shopping with my friends instead. We would arrange for one of our parents to drop us off at the Garden State Plaza and another to pick us up a few hours later. (My dad would always refuse at first and only step in to "save the day" when our plans were about to be ruined because we couldn't get a ride.) We'd try on overpriced hoodies and low-rise jeans at Abercrombie & Fitch and Hollister and buy heavily padded push-up bras and colorful thongs from Victoria's Secret.

My mom's objection to the items I coveted wasn't purely over the price tags. The popular girls at school wore silver Tiffany chokers with heart pendants. My mom didn't get it: "You're not a bulldog. Why would you want to wear a chain around your neck?"

The popular girls wore Juicy Couture tracksuits with "Juicy" written on the back. They had them in all different colors and patterns, pink and tie-dye, velour and terry cloth. My mom couldn't understand why I would want to wear anything made of a towel, in public, let alone draw attention to my butt.

Paris Hilton and Britney Spears and everyone at school wore UGGS. One girl, Kayla, had them in every pastel color from light pink and baby blue to lavender and lime green. I desperately wanted just one pair, the standard chestnut, but my mom didn't see the need to wear sheepskin fleeced boots to school. They were impractical, she said, not to mention hideous. There were loads of fakes, but I wanted the real thing with the real UGG label on the back.

I begged my mom to buy me a designer bag. Everyone had one. Naturally, my mom thought it ludicrous for an eleven-year-old girl to sport such a bag, to school of all places, until she saw for herself when she came to pick me up. It would be important for me to fit in. She bought me a gray handbag from Coach, which was hugely popular and the more affordable of the designer brands. I felt so proud going to school the next day with the signature Coach print on my shoulders. But I only had the one. The girls at my school took notice of how often you rotated your outfits, and the rich, popular girls swapped their designer handbags to match the day's outfit. To expand my wardrobe, I borrowed my mom's clothes and sometimes even her heels to school, even though they were too big for me.

~

72

I remember being in awe the first time we drove up to our house on Jane Drive. It was an all-American clapboard house on a quiet cul-de-sac, with a large front lawn and a two-car garage. The entrance to our driveway was flanked by lanterns and an American mailbox. We had a big island in the kitchen, a real fireplace, an in-house bar and a hot tub in the master bathroom. It was the biggest house we'd ever lived in. The government stipend didn't cover our rent, so my parents had to top it up.

The problem was that we were living in one of the richest neighborhoods in New Jersey, and some of my classmates lived in houses—mansions, really—with Georgian columns, horseshoe driveways, acres of lawns, grand marble kitchens, saunas and even indoor pools, on top of the outdoor ones. In comparison, our house didn't feel so impressive anymore. Even my parents referred to our neighbors' houses as "rich people's homes" and their dogs as "rich people's dogs." One of our neighbors had the most majestic, regal-looking dogs, always perfectly groomed, frolicking on their perfectly manicured lawn. It was a good thing I had to walk up the street to take the school bus.

Not long before, my family had been able to afford a comfortable expat life in Malaysia even though my dad was relatively junior. Thanks to the low cost of living, we had the help of a cleaner and never worried about the restaurant bill when eating out. My mom played tennis with a group of Chinese-Malay women and my dad played golf at the country clubs. I attended the international school, where our uniforms were the great equalizer. I'd never really thought about money.

But now, I resented being "poor." Not everyone at school was rich, and we sure weren't the "poorest," but I only ever compared myself to the richer kids because although being rich didn't guarantee popularity, it seemed to be a prerequisite. They seemed to have it all, the rich, white, popular kids. Even their parents were cool. Their moms wore Juicy tracksuits and drove Hummers and Range Rovers. My mom came to pick me up in her burgundy Kia Carnival minivan.

But there was another reason I didn't like my mom coming to school. To everyone else, it would have been obvious that I would have Asian parents. To me, it felt like she was blowing my cover: I was passing for white, until she ruined it.

~

I rarely experienced overt in-your-face racism, though occasionally kids pulled back their eyes, called me a "chink" or shouted "Ni hao ma" at me. Mostly I ignored it, though sometimes I'd give them the middle finger.

Some kids asked me where I was from. When I said Korea, they wanted to know if it was North or South. I've even been asked East or West.

"Do you speak Chinese there?"

"Are you related to Seung Lee [a classmate]?" I couldn't believe how ignorant they were.

"I heard you guys eat dogs."

I hated this one. "Eww, no!" I'd say, but I knew it was true. The older generation did eat bosintang, which literally translates to a soup to restore health. I never had it, but my grandpa once took my brother for a meal without telling him what it was. My brother, only a toddler then, complained the soup smelt like his pet dog in Rwanda.

I was terribly self-conscious about Korean food. At home, we would share boiling hot stews called jjigae and various banchan side dishes. The whole house stank when my mom cooked fish, pan-fried and served whole in the middle of the table to share. Using his chopsticks, my dad would adroitly work through the scaly body until only the skeleton was left. He would then gently press around the eyeball until the glazy marble thing popped out. Then the skeleton was flipped so the other eyeball could be extracted. I wished we could eat chicken and potatoes, or at least filleted fish, like "normal" white people. When we moved to Paris years later, I saw that the French too served their fish with eyes. It wasn't just the uncivilized, barbaric Asians, I thought. As if that made it more acceptable.

When my friends came over, I tried to avoid opening the fridge, worried the overpowering stench of kimchi might escape. For my first birthday in the US—I must have been turning twelve—I invited a group of girls over, and my mom prepared a lavish meal for us. I'm sure she went to different supermarkets to buy the freshest ingredients and spent days getting everything ready. My mom set the table beautifully in our formal dining room, which we rarely used, and brought out dishes of bulgogi, japchae glass noodles and spicy tteokbokki rice cakes. "Help yourselves, girls," she said, laying out different kinds of kimchi for my friends to try. But from the way they were looking at each other, I knew my friends didn't want to eat the smelly foreign foods. Ears aflame, I shot my mom a look to stop urging them to eat. We went up to play in my room, barely having touched the food. I wished we could order pizza like everyone else.

Later that afternoon, my mom drove us to the theater to watch *Anger Management*, the new Adam Sandler movie. She made us bags of popcorn at home so we wouldn't have to pay the extortionate theater prices. I was too embarrassed about lunch to enjoy the movie. The girls slept over afterwards and, the next day, my mom took us all to get our nails done as yet another birthday treat. This was more like it, though I hated the fact that the manicurists were Asian.

~

Unfortunately, I did well at school. I had to. Back in Malaysia, my dad had gone ballistic when my brother brought home a mixture of As and Bs in his grade report. It felt like the entire apartment was trembling. He said the same thing would happen to me if I ever got a B. Not long after that, I saw a C in my midterm report, in math of all subjects. Terrified, I asked to speak to my teacher after school. "My parents are going to kill me," I managed before breaking into sobs. Mr. Hing gently consoled me, then bumped up my grade to a B for the midterm on the promise that I would work hard for the rest of the year, which I did. My parents never found out, and mercifully I didn't get in trouble for the B.

To be honest, it didn't take much effort to be an all-A student in the US. The problem was, it was not cool to be smart. Everyone loved ditzy, like Paris Hilton in *The Simple Life*, Jessica Simpson in *Newlyweds* or Reese Witherspoon in

Legally Blonde. No one liked nerdy, especially not the Asian nerd. Since I couldn't do anything about my good grades or the fact that I was Asian, I needed some way to signal that I was different. On Saint Patrick's Day, I wore a green T-shirt that said "Kiss me, I'm Irish" on it. In class, I would ask silly questions. When our social sciences teacher explained that rubber was a plantation crop, like tea and coffee, I put my hand up and asked if that meant we could eat rubber. Another time, I was caught passing a note during math. "Hand it over," Ms. O'Connor said. After reading the note—"Ms. O'Connor has a camel toe"—she scrunched it up, threw it in the bin and gave me a detention.

I became progressively more rebellious. In sixth grade, I had no tardies and was unanimously praised by my teachers for "good behavior." I was still considered an "asset to class" in seventh grade, "an independent thinker" exhibiting "outstanding class performance," although it was noted that Lena "socializes excessively in class." However, by eighth grade, I had a grand total of thirty-three tardies and was spending an ever-increasing amount of time in detention.

≈

I was constantly trying not to be exposed. On the first day of school, my homeroom teacher asked that we all stand for this "pleja" something. I had no idea what she said, but everyone else seemed to know what to do. They stood from their seats, so I did too. They placed their right hand on their chest and faced the American flag in the top corner of the room, so I did the same. But then they all started mumbling something

I couldn't make out. It might as well have been a foreign language, a recital in Latin, a religious chant. I pretended to mouth something until it was all over and we sat down again, desperately hoping no one had noticed how lost I was.

I was surprised when the next day our teacher asked us to rise for that "pleja" thing again. And the next day, and the next. I thought it would only be for the first day of school. Eventually I found out that the teacher was saying Pledge of Allegiance and eventually I learned to recite it myself: "I pledge allegiance to the flag of the United States of America and to the Republic for which it stands, one nation under God, indivisible, with liberty and justice for all." I didn't understand what I was saying, but all I wanted was to fit in.

There were so many other slippery slopes, like cultural references going straight over my head. I hadn't watched *Friends*, *Seinfeld* or *The Simpsons*. I didn't recognize all fifty states, the famous US presidents, the key historical events. I didn't know the lyrics to "The Star-Spangled Banner" beyond "O say can you see." I worried most, though, about mispronouncing words.

In one English class, we took turns reading a passage out loud. I think it was from the dystopian novel *The Giver*. I counted the number of students before me and looked ahead to see which paragraph would land on me. Phew, there were no big words, nothing to trip me up.

"Lena, would you take the next one for us?"

"Sure," I said, and read confidently.

When I finished, a girl at my table quietly corrected me. "It's pronounced 'bin,' not 'bean.'"

Been. How could I get such an easy four-letter word

wrong? I felt humiliated. But for some reason, I insisted, "There's two Es in there, it's pronounced 'bean' like 'seen.'"

But I knew I'd been exposed, much like when you find yourself standing naked in the school corridor in a dream. Except this wasn't a dream.

11

Like many parents, my mom wanted for me what she didn't have herself, one of those being the ability and, perhaps more importantly, the confidence to dance. Hoping I might have more rhythm than her, she put me in a ballet class when I was a toddler and was happy to see her daughter tottering in a pink tutu. Little did she know I would enjoy it so much.

I loved performing—the costume, the spotlight, even the butterflies—and would go all out on stage. In Malaysia, my school club danced to Geri Halliwell's "It's Raining Men" and our dance teacher placed me right at the head of a pyramid formation. After the show, when Korean parents congratulated her, my mom beamed. "I don't know where she gets it from!" My mom was so proud she would happily sew shiny beads onto my costume, even though no one would be able to see the details from the audience.

When we moved to the US, I spent a good twelve hours a week at dance school, taking jazz, tap, ballet and lyrical classes. Once, I invited my friends Mary and Julia to my annual recital; my mom forced my dad and brother to come and support me too. It was a long program starting from the kiddies. At last, it was my turn.

I was still in full makeup with bright red lipstick and hair slicked back into a bun when I found my friends backstage. Mary and Julia hugged me tight and told me, "Well done, you were amazing." They kindly brought me a bouquet.

"What are we waiting for? Let's go now," my dad said as soon as he spotted us. My brother was there too, arms crossed, heels digging into the floor. I looked around, no one was leaving yet. The other dancers were being congratulated by their friends and family. I knew sitting through the recital would have been torturous for my dad, but couldn't he at least have pretended to be happy for me?

I nodded, pressing my lips tight. My mom quickly snapped a photo of me and my friends—I am choking on my tears in this photo—and we drove home in silence, Mary and Julia consoling me with a gentle stroke in the back row of our minivan. My dad only spoke to ask who needed to be dropped home first: Mary or Julia. I wished my mom had known better than to drag my dad and brother to the recital.

Maybe I couldn't blame him. It was my dad who picked me up from dance school on his way home from work, an hour-and-a-half journey already without the detour. But when his silver Hyundai Sonata approached, I would slouch into the front seat without even saying "hello" or making eye contact. It would be a thankless, silent twenty-minute drive home until the garage doors rumbled open. Then, slam.

My dad, sniffing up the stairs, would shout to my mom in a disappointed tone, "Is it kimchi jjigae again?"

"What do you mean 'again'? I just made it!" my mom would shout back.

81

"I had kimchi jjigae for lunch."

"How was I supposed to know that?"

My mom and dad bickered like this all the time. There were no big explosive fights; it was just kind of always there, like background noise. It seemed my mom was at fault for everything. Both my mom and dad would raise their voices, but it was always my dad who had the final say. When he had had enough, he would tell her to stop "talking back" at him—"What will the kids learn?" Even Jjanga knew who the head of the family was and tiptoed around his moods.

At home, no one asked how each other's day was. My dad was obviously at work, my brother and I were at school, and it was assumed my mom was up to banal chores. What was there to ask about doing the laundry, washing the dishes, picking up groceries, driving us to and from after-school activities?

It's also awkward to ask these basic questions in Korean. The Korean greetings are "*moh muh-guh-ssuh?*" (Have you eaten anything?) or "*mohae?*" (What are you up to?). You could ask "*jalissuh?*" (Have you been well?) to someone you haven't seen in a while, but I don't think the equivalents of "How are you?" or "How was your day?" exist. Even "*annyoung*" (Hello) doesn't quite feel right to say to your family.

We never said, "Thank you." I never thanked my dad for picking me up from dance school. No one thanked my mom for preparing a delicious meal, ever. But to say thank you in Korean ("*gomawo*"), especially to your parents, makes the relationship feel transactional. I think there is a degree of taking for granted what your parents would and should do for you in Korean (or perhaps Asian) families. Or maybe it was just my family.

It goes without saying we never said "I love you" to each other. I noticed my friends would say "Love you" or "Love you too" before hanging up the phone to their parents. But that was just not done in Korean families. "*Saranghae*" sounds romantic, not something you say to your family.

My family always spoke in Korean no matter where we lived. When abroad, my brother and I were sent to Korean school on Saturday mornings. It was important to my parents that my brother and I speak our native language fluently and not lose touch with our Korean heritage. Not normally one to judge, my mom would tut at other parents who let their kids forget their mother tongue. I, however, was envious of the kids whose parents didn't make them learn Korean or whose Korean was so poor they spoke with an American accent. But our statuses were different. They were immigrants, there to stay in America; we would be returning to Korea.

At school, I pretended not to speak Korean and avoided any association with the Korean kids. When I had to call my mom from school to ask if I could go over to a friend's, I would wander off to a safe distance, cup my mouth and whisper, even if I was out of earshot. The safest way to speak to her, though, was to pretend I needed the bathroom and get a hall pass during class. Even then, I checked the cubicles to make sure I was alone.

~

During seollal and chuseok, we would call both grandmas in Korea to say hello and pass the phone around. We carried on performing the ancestral rites, though we'd make do with an "abridged" version given it was just our nuclear family. Still, I remember my mom staying up late to skin raw chestnuts for the ancestral table. Because it was just the four of us, my brother and I would take turns offering the rice wine and placing the chopsticks in different dishes. "Your grandfather liked his roast chicken," my dad would say approvingly. Perhaps it made him feel like a dutiful son. Perhaps he was setting an example for me and my brother. Sometimes he would say things like, "Please let Seung Gon and Lena become obedient children." *Whatever.*

I hated performing these rituals and hoped no one at school would find out. I wished we could celebrate the "normal" holidays like Christmas and Thanksgiving. Other than a fake Christmas tree, which in fairness my mom decorated beautifully each year, we had no Christmas tradition to speak of. We had no special Christmas meal. We had no family to visit or invite. We never exchanged gifts, or if we did, it would have been something practical bought months before where my mom would say, "This is your Christmas present." I believe my first pair of glasses, the silver-rimmed ones, were technically a Christmas present.

~

My brother and I shared a computer room where we each had one of those giant PCs and thick monitors. I would be busy instant messaging my friends, while he played computer games, I think *StarCraft*. We mostly kept to ourselves, though I could hear him clicking ferociously, grunting, sighing and occasionally swearing at his dark screen with alien characters and laser beams.

When dinner was ready, my mom rang her handbell from the kitchen to avoid shouting. I usually went down promptly and helped set the table or serve the rice, in order: a big mound for my dad, a slightly smaller one for my brother, then a half portion for me. My mom always insisted on serving herself last.

"Seung Gonnnn!!!" My mom would end up having to shout anyway. It was obvious my brother was finishing up his computer game. I hated the fact that he never helped in the house unless explicitly ordered to do so, and even then, in a big grouch.

I knew what to expect from my parents at dinner. "Seung Gon, you're in high school. Are you even thinking about college? What are you going to do with the rest of your life? Stop wasting your time." My brother would talk back aggressively. There was such anger in his eyes. After dinner, he would go right back to the computer room and resume his gaming. I wished I had a different brother.

My brother used to be athletic. In Korea, he was the fastest sprinter in his class and played in the school tennis championship. He played basketball and soccer and was always breaking one bone or another. When we came to the US, he signed up for his school's track and field team. The trouble was, he might have been fast in Korea, but wasn't fast enough to compete with the black and white kids in America. Even I was sometimes teased that Asians were only good at ping pong, and my only comeback was that we had the brains. This kind of thing must have been confidence-destroying for a high school boy. I wonder if he turned to computer games because he couldn't find connection elsewhere. He'd had many Korean friends in Malaysia but seemed to have few friends in Franklin Lakes, possibly because there were few Koreans.

I don't think he had any girlfriends either. It must have been difficult for him being in a predominantly white town when Asian guys were (and are) routinely emasculated and desexualized. Perversely, I took part in that. I remember doing this thing of pressing my thumb and index finger together and opening it just barely half an inch. Then I'd squint as if to peer through and pull a face at my brother.

"Fuck off," he'd say. It was a surefire way to wind him up.

"Don't bother, Seung Gon," my dad would intervene. "The smaller pepper is spicier."

"Yeah, Seung Gon, the smaller pepper is spicier," I'd taunt in a singsong voice.

More than anything, I think it says a lot about my own preoccupations at the time.

12

When we lived in Malaysia, my parents bought my brother a Walkman and me a portable CD player, along with my first CD, Christina Aguilera's self-titled debut. Headphones on, I turned up the volume and sang along to "What a Girl Wants" and "Genie in a Bottle." I had no idea I could sing so well. I sang louder and louder until my brother shouted at me to shut up. Only when I pulled one headphone out did I realize why he was so irritated.

One dance class around that time, all the girls huddled in one corner of the room to do across-the-floor routines. As I waited for my turn, I smelled something was off and sniffed around. The source of the noxious smell turned out to be very close: my own armpits. That was the first time I became aware of my own body odor.

It wouldn't be long before my emerging self-awareness turned into full-blown self-consciousness. When we moved to the US, my biggest insecurity was being Asian. I hated what I saw in the mirror: my big head, my flat face, my small eyes. I would hold up a mirror to inspect my profile in the bathroom and pinch the shallow ridge of my nose to see what I would look like with a more Western nose.

I started noticing my facial and body hair. I hated my black mustache. I tweezed my eyebrows thinner and thinner. I wanted to shave my legs like my friends did, but my mom said they would only end up growing thicker. So I tweezed each hair, one by one, believing taking it out by the roots would mean they wouldn't grow back thicker.

I hated my legs. The other girls, especially the popular girls, had long, lean legs. I had my mom and dad's short, stocky legs. All the Abercrombie jeans were too long for me and had to be taken in. The worst was my calves. It looked like a baseball had been stitched inside each leg. My ankles were thick and my feet fat and stubby like my dad's.

No boy would find me attractive. Boys liked blondes and brunettes, maybe redheads. But there wasn't even a category for someone like me: a blackhead? There was one black Victoria's Secret Angel—Tyra Banks—but not a single Asian one. Asians simply weren't attractive.

~

Each semester we had a school dance in our canteen-cum-auditorium, an important social event in the middle school calendar. My friends and I would get ready together at someone's house, putting on our best push-up bras and asking each other how our butts looked in different outfits. As we did each other's hair and makeup, I felt self-conscious that I didn't have eyelids like my friends to put different shades of eyeshadow on. And even though my hair was straight, I used a straightener like them. We would check ourselves out in the mirror, smacking our lips, always perfectly glossy from a squeeze of Juicy Tube.

We danced provocatively, forming circles and grinding each other, not particularly bothered by the teachers who were chaperoning but looking over our shoulders to see if anyone was watching our moves. To Snoop Dogg's "Drop It Like It's Hot," we popped our butts, just like in the music video. When Nelly sang, "It's gettin' hot in here," we lifted our tops above our belly buttons. We danced and sang along to "Candy Shop," oblivious to the blatant misogyny of 50 Cent giving us permission to "lick the lollipop."

At one of many sleepovers at Mary's, a group of us girls sat in a circle on her bed. We kissed in pairs and gave each other constructive feedback: "You should try to wag your tongue less" or "Maybe a little less slimy?" All in our train-track braces.

In eighth grade, we started experimenting with boys. You didn't want to be a prude. Or worse, a slut. You wanted to be "experienced." Once, a bunch of us were hanging out in a friend's basement and blindfolded the one boy who was with us. The girls took turns stroking him over his shorts, and he had to guess whose hand it was. It was the first time I felt a penis with my hands.

I had felt one on my body before. It was in the science classroom after school. The lights were off. No one was around. I was flirting with one of the popular boys, who playfully pushed me against the teacher's desk at the front. I tried to lean away but in doing so pushed my pelvis forward and could feel his unmistakable boner on my belly.

~

In our reception room, we had a fancy lacquered drinks trolley with a few bottles of hard liquor, which my parents didn't seem to take notice of. One night when I had a group of friends over, we snuck my dad's Chivas Regal into my room upstairs. We each took a sip straight from the bottle, squirming as the whisky stung our throats, and passed it around. My mom came to bring us some apples, but she didn't notice a thing. The creaking stairs gave us ample warning to hide the bottle.

I was thirteen when I got drunk off my face for the first time. Julia and I were sleeping over at another friend Emily's and we took big swigs straight from a bottle of Bacardi Emily had managed to procure, likely also from her parents' stash, not giving any time for the alcohol to kick in. The room started spinning and spinning and spinning; we were just having so much fun. Then we heard footsteps coming up the stairs.

"What's going on up there?" It was Emily's mom.

"Pretend you're sleeping, quick, quick," Emily whispered as she frantically hid the bottle.

I lay prostrate on the floor and passed out before being jolted awake only a moment later by someone picking me up from under my arms.

It was Emily's older brother, who also came to check on us. "They're drunk!" he cried.

To my great relief, Emily's mom didn't say anything to my mom when she came to pick me up the next morning.

Once we started drinking, it became obvious that more alcohol meant more fun. But whenever we drank, I seemed to drink more than everyone else. Not only was I having

90

more fun, but it also felt like I was more fun to be around. I often blacked out but loved hearing the stories and laughing at my own antics the next day.

13

Saying goodbye hadn't been such a big deal when I left Malaysia. Being at an international school where people came and went all the time, farewells were a ritual process. We signed each other's yearbooks and scribbled we-will-miss-you's on our uniform shirts. We hugged and we waved. No one cried, I don't think.

Well, I'm not sure anymore how upset or distressed I was. I've moved so many times since, and subsequent goodbyes would be much more poignant, so when I think back to all the farewells over time, the one in Malaysia pales in comparison. But I may well be downplaying how I felt at the time, I don't know.

It was different when I had to leave the US. I'm not sure when I found out we were moving back to Korea. We'd done two overseas postings, three years each, so it was time, but back then I didn't know our moves had such a regular cadence. My parents always kept it vague, probably to keep me focused on whatever country we were living in. "We don't know until we know," they would say. Then one day my dad would have received the official reassignment. We had three months left.

My parents never seemed to have been good at managing my expectations. When my dad was posted to the UN the first time, when I was a little over two, they left me behind to stay with my grandma in Korea while they settled in. My brother, who was six then, went with them. As for me, I woke up one morning to find my parents missing. "Where's Umma and Appa?" I asked my grandma.

"They left for America this morning," she said. "They tried to wake you, but you were fast asleep, so they left without you."

My grandma says my two-year-old face turned into a look of total shock and abandonment. It might explain why I've been a light sleeper ever since. For a month, my grandma would point to planes in the sky and count the days until we left for "*migook*" (America). My grandma tells me, "The morning we were due to fly, I felt something on my face. I opened my eyes, it was still dark out, and there you were, stroking my face in the moonlight, making sure I wouldn't leave you behind."

This time, I wished my parents would leave me behind. Everyone else at school would be moving on to one of three high schools in the area. That's what all my friends were talking about, the pros and cons of each school and who was going where. I wished I could go to high school with them, though I knew that would never happen.

On the last day of school, we signed each other's yearbooks: *HAGS* (which apparently stands for "have a good summer"). *I'll miss you. Stay in touch. XOX.*

I got to attend graduation. This was the only time I'd completed a full chunk of my education in one place, all three years of middle school, from start to finish. It was a beautiful summer's day. I wore a light purple satin dress and had my hair and makeup done. When the ceremony started, my dad got out of his seat and inched up the aisle to take good photos of me. I gave him the "What are you doing? Stop embarrassing me and go back to your seat" look. I was sure all the kids could see him, and it was obvious whose parent he was. I am frowning in every photo my dad took.

After graduation, my friends organized a going away party for me. It was at Julia's, and someone brought a big bottle of vodka. Everyone took sips, but I took gulps. I wanted to get drunk and got very drunk, very fast.

We all slept over at Mary's on my last night. I forget what we talked about. Maybe we reminisced about the good times, maybe we shared our anxiety about the future and the big transition to high school. No doubt there was some chat about boys.

These were my best friends. BFFs. After sharing everything for three years, we were inseparable. We studied together, danced together, shopped together, laughed together, got drunk together. We were silly together, jumping on the trampoline, making prank calls, ding dong ditching. We were reckless, spontaneous and mischievous. We were growing up together.

The dreaded moment came when my mom came to pick me up the following morning. I sulked in the backseat and pulled down the window. My friends huddled around, leaning into the car. We said our final goodbye. They tried to hold on as my mom gently stepped on the accelerator. It was like a hearse driving away. My friends wept, and it felt like a part of me really had died.

PART THREE

Coming "Home"

2005–2014

14

SEOUL, KOREA, 2005 (age 14)

I have this strange feeling every time I return to Korea. On the drive in from Incheon airport, I pass endless stretches of high-rise apartments, elderly women waiting at bus stops, children chasing one another around. It's a familiar scene, but I'm hit with the "realization" that while I was busy living my life abroad, there was a parallel life, as real and continuous as mine, taking place in Korea. There is nothing out of the ordinary. Everyone is going about their lives, as they were. To me, it feels like a time warp.

I was coming back after six years abroad. I had been to Korea during that time, but only as a visitor who would return "home" to Malaysia and then to the US. This time, I was here to stay. I was coming "home-home," to my passport country, the place I was born, where I'd gone to elementary school and where all my extended family lived. But I stood out. There were telltale signs like my tan, my short shorts, my Coach handbag, my slight American accent when I spoke in Korean.

My brother and I flew back first, while my parents finished packing up, and we stayed with my grandma—her house always served as our transitional home when we were in between countries. I felt relieved to see her again, especially after the way my grandpa had died so unexpectedly. You just never knew. She had downsized significantly but still had the hanging scroll of a tiger at the entrance, to ward off any misfortune; the trinkets and souvenirs my grandpa liked to collect from his travels, including mummy jars containing unidentifiable things; and a set of wall-to-wall black lacquer armoires with a mother-of-pearl inlay of birds and flowers. My grandma was glad to have us back. She was still cooking galbijjim for us and pushing banchan plates in front of me and my brother.

It felt like I was resuming the "on" phase of an on-and-off long-distance relationship with my extended family. When my well-meaning aunt, Emo, kept hiking up my bra straps, looking out for my modesty, I shirked my shoulders to get her hands off me. Who cared if my bra straps showed? She constantly remarked how much I'd changed ("You used to love eating tteokbokki!"), almost sounding disappointed, not remembering I was eight when I had left Korea. I was fourteen now.

Emo was more than twenty years older than me but more like a friend than an adult. She hadn't married, which she blamed on the weight she had gained—close to 20 kilos in the time we'd been abroad. I couldn't truthfully say to her, "You haven't changed one bit!" Emo confided to me that she now smoked—always in private as it was frowned upon for women to smoke in public. She carried in her wallet a photo of herself from university, still thin and pretty and surrounded by a pack of boys. "That's me there," she would say. She spent too much time wondering what could have been, and without children of her own, she projected her maternal feelings onto me.

Over that summer, Emo taught me how to text and say the Korean equivalents of "lol" and "omg." She gave me a crash course on Korean pop culture, pointing out the names of celebrities I should be aware of. Kim Tae-hee was considered one of the most beautiful women in Korea, known for her pale skin, "egg-shaped" face and wide-slit eyes. I just couldn't see it. After six years abroad, my beauty standards had become more Western than Asian. When I saw billboards advertising whitening creams and women shielding themselves with visors, I remembered tanning on the roof with Julia and getting in trouble when my mom pulled into the driveway ("Get off the roof, now!"). In the West, a tan symbolized the luxury of a beach holiday; in Korea, a tan was the byproduct of laboring in the fields.

Emo introduced me to the hit TV series *My Lovely Sam Soon*, a kind of Korean *Bridget Jones's Diary*. Apart from the clichéd storyline, it was the Koreanness of it all that I found most cringeworthy. The kiss scenes were so PG—they barely pressed their lips together. But I was hooked. In one famous scene, Sam Soon wears a towel rolled into the shape of a ram's horns on her head. To recreate this iconic "sheep head" scene, Emo took me to a *jjimjilbang*. I had been to these public bathhouses when I was younger and knew what to expect, but I no longer wanted to strip naked in front of strangers. So, I changed into my bikini. As we dipped our toes in the warm bath, one of the "aunties" who worked there came over, her udder-like breasts on full display, and told me to take my bikini off.

"Why do you want to see me naked?" I said, giving her a dirty look.

"Do you see anyone else wearing anything in here? Take it off or get out."

"Pervert," I mumbled under my breath.

After reluctantly giving in, I tried to cover myself with a small towel as we moved between baths, from warm to hot to cold. Some women were exfoliating themselves with scrubbing mitts, sitting on miniature plastic stools. Emo asked if I wanted to get a professional scrub by one of the aunties. "No thanks," I said. We changed into some loose-fitting T-shirts and shorts and hopped between the kiln sauna and ice room in the unisex area. We lounged on massage chairs, snacked on baked eggs and tried to roll our towels on our head, just like Sam Soon.

Later at university, I would learn that anthropologists have a three-phase structure for rites of passage or life events that mark significant transitional periods like birth, puberty, marriage and death. Looking back, I recognize the three phases—separation, transition and reincorporation—in each of my moves. When I first returned to Korea, I was in the transitional phase, which is also called a period of liminality where you are "no longer" and simultaneously "not yet." That's exactly how I felt: I was no longer a part of American society but not yet a part of Korean society either.

My mom returned to Korea a few weeks later and brought me a letter from Mary, along with some photos from our last days together. Mary told me about her summer in Illinois, how she dreaded going to high school with no friends, how Julia wasn't even in any of her classes. She begged me to come back somehow.

I wanted to go back as much as Mary wanted me to come back. It had only been a few weeks, but we were worlds apart. Korea and the US were like night and day, literally. We were over 10,000 kilometers apart and fourteen time zones away.

~

Returning to Korea meant misalignment of academic years, again. In Korea, the academic year is aligned with the calendar year, which always made more sense to me, and the school years are grouped differently. I had just graduated from middle school, so should have started ninth grade, the first year of high school in the US. In Korea, however, ninth grade is the last year of middle school. Even more awkwardly, moving in the summer meant I would join in the middle of an academic year, for one semester. My parents, however, thought it would be an excellent opportunity for me to acclimatize before I started high school the following February. "Just try it out," my mom said.

On the first day of school, the teacher introduced me as the new kid from America and everyone clamored for me to speak in English. Looking around sheepishly in my new hand-me-down uniforms, I relented and gave a quick introduction. The classroom stirred; a few kids imitated my pronunciation. "Say something else," they shouted. News spread down the hall and students came to catch a glimpse of this new girl during breaks. I had no idea speaking English would be such a big deal. I didn't want to look like I was showing off, so made sure to pronounce the loanwords the

Korean way, like "hem-buh-guh" and "cum-pyoo-tuh."

Even though I started school knowing I would only be there for one semester, I was keen to make new friends. To my relief, the girls—it was a girls' school—were welcoming and invited me to lunch. Everything about me seemed to fascinate them, even the way I tied my hair into a messy bun at the top of my head—like a topknot, they said. They affectionately called me "butthole panties" because I wore thongs. They giggled when I made some mistakes in Korean, like when I tried to say, "shut my eyes," the literal translation sounded like I had door handles on my eyes. Or when I said, "make my bed," it was as if I was manufacturing a bed.

To me, everything and everyone seemed just so "Korean"—in a bad way. Everyone looked the same, straight black hair with bangs. They dressed the same, in the school uniform with a pair of Converse. I couldn't get over how stereotypically Korean my classmates were. They posed with the peace sign in photos. They held hands and linked arms when walking down corridors. (I learned this kind of intimate, non-sexual touching between friends is called "*skinship*"—the word itself is Konglish, a fusion of English and Korean words, which Koreans are often surprised to learn are not proper English words.) They were obsessed with the boy band Dong Bang Shin Ki, literally the "Rising Gods of the East," who to me looked like a group of five effeminate guys. In three years of being surrounded by white people, I had turned into a "banana": yellow on the outside but white on the inside. It would take many years to undo the damage from such internalized racism acquired during my most formative years.

My classmates wanted to know what school was like in America. Had I ever kissed a boy? They sat around, asking me to tell more. Where did I even begin for kids who hadn't even had their first kiss? I thought them prudish and inexperienced. When I told them about getting drunk with my friends and kissing boys, their eyes bulged and mouths dropped. I hoped to get up to similar fun here, but I knew it wouldn't go down well. There were two girls in my class who drank and hung out with boys outside of school, and they were considered unsavory characters.

When I first moved back to Korea, I would call Mary and Julia from my grandma's landline and tell them how bizarre my new school was. My mom later told me that the phone bill came to over the equivalent of a hundred dollars, but my grandma didn't want to stop me. But the calls became less frequent—Mary and Julia were also starting at their new high school—until one day they stopped. "Keep in touch," even when spoken with the most sincerity, was much easier said than done.

~

While I navigated Korean middle school culture, my parents evaluated the best high school for me. As in previous moves, I was oblivious; I would go to whatever school my parents put me in. Really, it was my mom's decision. Her philosophy in every country we lived in was that I should get as local and authentic an experience as possible.

I started hearing more about this thing called *wehgo*. Wehgo is a type of private school that literally means foreign language high school, so-called for its heavy emphasis on English (though the primary language of instruction is Korean) and a second language such as Japanese and Chinese or French and German. I didn't realize at the time that middle school students were preparing night and day to enter these hyper-competitive schools. Before I knew it, I was in the admissions game too. The one I would be applying to was called Myongji, a mid-league wehgo recommended by my mom's friend whose daughter was studying there. Wasn't the moms' network the best source of information?

To prepare for the entrance exams, I was sent to *hagwon*, the notorious private institution for after-school and weekend tuition, a pervasive part of Korean education. I had gone to hagwon in elementary school, but back then it was mostly for fun stuff, like swimming lessons, though my mom did also put me in a philosophy hagwon. I wrote in my second-grade journal:

Philosophy is boring. Why do people study philosophy? Is it to help them think? If there's philosophy for children, does that mean there's philosophy for adults? Isn't playing outside more important for kids than studying philosophy?

Amen to my seven-year-old self.

The stakes were much higher now. The best hagwons were in Gangnam, which literally means south of the river, and we lived well north. The sad irony was that my mom was driving me all the way to Gangnam so that I could listen to a tape of a conversation conducted in English and answer multiple-choice questions testing my understanding of the dialogue. I told my mom this was ludicrous, but she made me carry on anyway. I hate to think of all the time and money wasted on hagwon, but this would only be the start.

I didn't make much of it when I was accepted at Myongji given I had applied via a special route for English competency. But I should have known better from the way my new friends were reacting. My name was listed on a banner outside my middle school gate, along with some other students who had been accepted to other wehgo.

A few weeks before starting at Myongji, I wrote in my journal (in Korean):

Dec 19, 2005. It's been just over five months since I came back from the US. Time passes so, so fast. I suppose it's because there's so much I want to do and have to do. I'm not sure if I like Korea or the US more. In the US, I played every weekend. In Korea, I'm always studying, but it's not so bad. But I am getting really stressed. Homework for my private lessons, homework for Myongji. It's driving me crazy. Sometimes I really want to die. I'm tired of doing homework and studying all the time. I'm tired of studying after school every day. They say it'll be worth it when I'm older, but even then, I'll be going to work every day. I'm not sure why I'm alive. It would be easy to be dead. It's probably fear because no one really knows what it means to die.

15

Myongji had mandatory boarding for all. The school's philosophy is explained in an old brochure I found recently in a cardboard box. It says the school is not a building but a "software" to build your academics and character: "a professional operating system to allow you to study and live in an environment as comfortable as home." Under this system, a student can self-study for a maximum of 394,200 minutes over a three-year period. However, students are "too young to manage themselves." Studying together in the library can alleviate their fight against themselves, their fight against "game, sleep and idleness." Having eighty students per superintendent allows for "individual attention, protection and love."

It goes on to say: "If you have clear goals in life, studying becomes a means to an end, which will enhance your learning efficiency." It's a strange idea to promote—turning studying into a means to an end rather than something inherently worthwhile—but it epitomizes the mentality underlying the Korean education system.

So how did the school go about maximizing our potential to study 394,200 minutes?

~

It's 8 a.m. and my woefully incompetent homeroom teacher is flirting with the class 9 boys, as usual, flicking her shiny black hair that comes down to her waist. Class 9 is not an actual class—there are only eight classes in each year—but a kind of splinter group within my class of six boys who are taller and more athletic, too cool for everyone else. One of them is short and weedy but makes the cut because he is a year older. Out of respect, the other boys call him *hyung*, rather than by his name. As a group, they are disruptive and often bully the other boys. I don't know who came up with it, but the name stuck, even teachers and parents calling them class 9. "Okay then, I will see you at the end of the day," my homeroom teacher says in her shrill voice.

First up is math. Our teacher is a lanky, dry, bespectacled man who comes in on the bell, picks up a chalk and starts his lesson from the top left corner of the board. Every now and again, he turns to face us and asks, "Is everyone following?" He should really be asking, "Is anyone following?" I feel narcoleptic. I physically can't keep my eyes open. It's not just me. A few heads fall during class, then a few more, as if a sleeping bug is spreading. It's common for students to sleep with their heads on their desks during class. Many of us have dolls or cushions in the classroom to use as pillows. Boys protectively place these on their laps when they are dozing off. Some teachers send us to the standing desks at the back of the classroom, but our math teacher chuckles as he sees he is losing most of us. He leaves on the bell and a classmate brushes the board.

Every other class is English: English grammar, English reading comprehension, English composition, English conversation. We are taught when to use definite versus indefinite articles (a particular challenge for Koreans as there are no articles in the Korean language), what a relative clause is (I still can't say), sentence structures like "many + a/an + singular verb." *Many an hour was wasted on English class.* We are tested on the differences between "lie lied lay laid lain," something even native speakers get wrong all the time. I don't like any of my teachers and only ever pay attention to give them a hard time. Twice a week, we have English conversation class, which is taught by a native speaker, always white and American, the race and accent preferred by Korean parents—ideal for brochures.

We have two hours of PE per week in our first year. In the second year, this is reduced to one so that we can focus on the important subjects. One mom in my class wants to replace this one hour of PE with self-study time. Why waste an hour on physical health when every hour of study counted? Surely it was detracting from the 394,200 minutes.

At the end of the school day, after six pointless lessons, our homeroom teacher is back, click-clacking in her heels. She loves to pick on the non-class 9 boys. "Gwangho, you're on mopping duty again," she says, looking to curry favor with the class 9 boys, who roar with laughter.

Then the other half of our day starts.

We "self-study" at our desks until the dinner bell rings at 6:10 p.m. The classroom doors are kept open, and a teacher patrols the corridors.

Dinner is served in the canteen, on the ground floor of the school building. A typical meal consists of rice, soup, a meat and two banchan side dishes. We're allowed back in the dormitory to change out of the school uniform and into our activewear: either bright orange T-shirts lined with white collars or light blue polo shirts with lime green stripes for boys and orange stripes for girls. Chic!

After dinner, we report to our seats in the library, which is adjacent to the dorm. The rooms are bare except for rows of partitioned workstations. Some students have tacked on motivational Post-it notes, *"Carpe diem"* being a popular one. Others have calendars with the countdown to D-Day, the next big exam. A set of superintendents roam the libraries checking off student names from a clipboard, while another inspects the dorm, room by room. They communicate with each other on walkie-talkies.

There is a points system. You are given points for not being at your desk, points for being late, points for chatting, points for hiding in the closet or under the duvet when the inspectors come around. Periodically everyone with points is summoned to the gymnasium to be disciplined in a kind of boot camp. We hold planks and do jumping jacks. We go around in circles in a deep squat position while pinching our earlobes with each hand. Every half-hour, everyone with up to five incremental points is dismissed. I have to stay until the end.

At 9 p.m., everyone flocks to the canteen to collect their snacks. Some boys play soccer; some girls walk in circles around the field.

By 9:30 p.m., we are back in the library for our final two-hour session.

At 11:30 p.m., the bell rings. We are allowed back to the dorm. Lights out at midnight.

Music blares through the sound system. I'm on the top bunk, so the speaker is blasting into my ears. I groan and smother myself under my pillow. It's 6:20 a.m. I can hear the muffled sounds of my roommates getting up. There's eight of us in our shoebox dorm. I stay in bed as long as I can.

The entire school convenes on the sports field. Some are still in their pajamas. Boys have hair sticking out in all directions. It's cold and still dark, but kids need discipline. We're ordered from first to third grade, classes 1 to 8. We stand in pairs and start counting. "One!" the first two shout and squat; "Two!" the next two shout and squat, and so on. There's always a few missing. More points!

A superintendent starts doing exercises at the podium to some uplifting music. Uh-one, two, three, four. He's stretching his arms in circles, lunging right and left. Half-asleep, we follow his moves. The exercise is brief, probably less time than it took us to do the roll call. We can now return to our dorms, all nine hundred of us making our way back in.

To be fair, we don't do this every morning. The superintendents are still working it out. It's a young school and I'm only in the third intake. We'll do these early morning exercises for a few weeks, then it is scrapped, until it is reinstated a few months later in another form.

Eight girls getting ready in one bathroom is a logistical nightmare, so I use the communal showers at the end of the corridor. I go wrapped in a towel, shower basket in hand. Sometimes there is a queue, which is awkward for everyone.

There are no curtains or dividers, just shower heads fixed along each wall. I quickly wash my hair. I never get used to pooing in the communal toilets, though. Constipation is a real problem.

I get dressed into my uniform: white shirt, ready-made tie, dark gray vest and an A-line skirt that comes just below my knees, a wholly unflattering look for my overdeveloped calves. I throw on the matching dark gray jacket with my name tag on.

After breakfast, I trudge up the stairs to our classroom. And the day starts again.

We can go home on Saturdays. Around lunchtime, the sports field turns into a parking lot as parents come to pick up their children. You can count on the Saturday lunch menu to be a treat. The portions are bigger too, food heaped on our trays by the canteen ladies. I'm happy to be picked up, even if I'm going to be dropped right back off the next day.

Most students go to hagwon on the weekends, for Korean, English and math lessons. My mom drives me straight to a dance school in Gangnam. It's not like in the US, where we wore leotards and did across-the-floor exercises in a group. In Korea, such classes only exist for serious, professional dancers. I have a two-hour private lesson where I learn the choreography to popular K-pop songs. The other moms think my mom is out of her mind, letting me go to dance school of all places. Not only is it a distraction from my studies, but dance is perceived as an unwholesome activity.

After my dance lessons, I have private tuition with

university students looking to make some spare cash, then spend the rest of the weekend catching up on sleep.

On Sunday evening, my mom drives me back for another week of incarceration.

~

I often wondered what high school was like for Mary and Julia, and if they still thought about me. Just a few months earlier, I was going to the mall, jumping on the trampoline and hanging out in the pizza parlor with them after school. Now here I was, trapped in this hyper-regimented school, with a total lack of personal space, any meaningful exercise or extracurricular activities.

Directly behind our dormitory there was a juvenile detention center. It had the same layout as our school: concrete buildings arranged in an L-shape around a sand field, all protected by wire fences. Sometimes we would see kids playing outside in their prison tracksuits. Our lives didn't seem all that different to me. We were given numbers like an inmate's ID. Mine was 1436: I was in the first grade, class 4, number 36. We were locked in, doing the same thing day after day, going from the school to the library to the dormitory. Every day was the same. We were, in a way, serving our time: three years. The sheer monotony of living this day in and day out drove me crazy.

Of course, not everyone felt this way. Most students had worked incredibly hard to make it to Myongji. This is exactly what they had signed up to: the routine, the structure, the discipline. They had been conditioned all their lives to expect this. Pretty much from birth, Koreans are taught to shoot for the SKY, the triumvirate of Korean universities: Seoul, Korea and Yonsei. If you fell short of the SKY, you were to aim for a second-tier or at least an "in-Seoul" university. You were a failure if you went to a regional university. (The one exception is KAIST, known as the MIT of Korea, where my brother studied. I rarely saw him during this time as I was at boarding school, and KAIST is a two-and-a-half-hour drive south of Seoul.) It is accepted that the name of your university will follow you for the rest of your life, either as a trophy or a tarnish, and your entire future—job, salary, marriageability—hinged on it. A student should, therefore, behave like a student. Meaning, no distractions.

Every other week or so—they never told you when—the prefects stood outside the school looking you up and down, ready to call you out. Hey you, tuck your shirt in. Where's your tie? Go put your name tag on. Slippers not allowed. No makeup or jewelry.

Girls were supposed to have their hair neat and tidy in a ponytail, though we usually got away with having it down as long as it wasn't dyed or permed. There was one incident, though, when a quiet girl went in early to study. Our music teacher was checking each classroom to ensure no one had evaded the inspections. He found his prey. Noting there was nothing else to fault, he demanded she put her hair up. But she didn't have a hair tie. And you call yourself a student? He shoved her head against the wall.

This teacher was notorious, and he was fired not long after this incident. I'd had my palms caned by him too, for refusing to sing in front of the classroom as part of our midterm exams. Corporal punishment was not like in the olden days where students were battered and bruised, but it was still tolerated. Some teachers carried around a disciplinary stick, dubbed the "stick of love," even if it was only used as a pointer.

Boys were supposed to keep their hair nice and trim since long hair would distract them from their studies. Of course, this meant boys clung to their hair for life, taking special pride in their sideburns, as if they were Hasidic Jews. Historically, Korean men had topknots as cutting your hair was considered a sin. Confucius said our hair was a gift from our parents and should be treated as such. There is even a saying, "I'd rather cut my neck before my hair." Then, Gojong, the last king of Joseon and later the first emperor of Korea, introduced the Haircutting Act in 1895, requiring men to cut their hair short, among other radical "modernizing" reforms. While Gojong cut his own hair short, followed by top officials and military men, the act was met with widespread revolt by the commoners. Inspectors were stationed at busy areas and threatened to cut off topknots with their scissors. Some men killed themselves. More than a hundred years later, their sacrifices would come in handy for the schoolboys who wanted to keep their hair long in the name of filial piety.

Freedom of hairstyle was a real issue of basic human rights being discussed right up in the top echelons of government. Our school brought in hairdressers who forcibly cut boys' hair in the gymnasium. It was reported in the news that teachers had cut the students' hair themselves at several schools. All in the name of: "A student should behave like a student." I simply couldn't understand why schools would need to crack down on individual hairstyles.

The obsession with university admissions starts early, but really comes to a head in high school, the three most critical years of your life. By the time you're a senior, called a *gosam*, you should look like a zombie. You shouldn't be seeing friends, God forbid dating. You are not expected at family gatherings. You should be fat, constipated and full of acne.

One fateful November day, over half a million gosam students all over Korea sit *suneung*, eight back-to-back hours of standardized exams. Ahead of the big day, parents and grandparents pray at Buddhist temples, bowing a hundred times in front of golden Buddhas. The stock markets open late on the day; planes are grounded to minimize noise. In the early morning, first- and second-year students come out holding up "good luck" posters and handing out sticky sweets called *yuht* to help them "stick" to the university of their choice. If that day in November is not a good day, the students might need to lock themselves up in a *gosiwon* and re-sit the following year and maybe even the year after.

It's all about deferred gratification. Just focus on your studies now. You'll get to do everything once you get into a good university. You can go shopping, go to the movies, lose weight, get plastic surgery and even date. It will be all the sweeter then. Just trust us.

Meanwhile, they tell us school days are the best days of our lives.

114

16

I tried to do well at school, I really did. I would do practice test after practice test and did in fact do alright in workbooks, but being at a wehgo, our exams were much more difficult than the standard curriculum. As much as I tried, it was guesswork during exams, especially in math. My exam strategy was to decide whether to go all-in on one option or stagger my answers down the bubble sheet.

Instead of getting an A, B, C or D, we were labeled—like grades of cattle—from rank 1 to 9. The top 4 percent were rank 1; the middle was distributed in the shape of a diamond, with the middle 20 percent in rank 5; the bottom 4 percent were rank 9. Across subjects like history, math and Korean literature, I was consistently in rank 9, the bottom 4 percent of my year.

I felt like a failure, like low-grade cattle. It felt worse because I was trying. After six years abroad, studying in Korean felt like I was learning a new language. During self-study sessions, I would look up every other word in my Sharp dictionary, only to have to look up another word because I didn't understand the definition. Was it possible to be dyslexic in one language? That's what it felt like. Korean letters were so tightly spaced they gave me a headache. There was no point wrestling. Studying was clearly not for me.

Almost overnight, I went from being an effortless all-A student to pretty much the bottom of my class. If in America I acted ditzy to compensate for my good grades, there was no such need in Korea. How could I compete with students who'd topped their schools, who'd been going to hagwon religiously, not only for revision but to "study ahead" so that they were already familiar with the material when it was taught at school? Nothing could have prepared me, not the Saturday schools when I was abroad, the summer trips back to Korea, the private tuition to keep up with the level of math in Korea, not even the few transitional months at my new middle school.

Apart from my confidence and sense of self-worth being annihilated, I hated the excessive focus on grades at the expense of true learning. The first article I chose for one of our weekly newspaper journaling assignments was titled, "A+ A+ A+ Grade Inflation at Universities." I wrote (in Korean):

From the moment we are born, it seems all Korean kids do is study. My four-year-old cousin takes private lessons for Korean and math every day. Even in university, it's all about your grades. If you look at other countries, especially in the West, they don't work like us and they live just fine. Why do we have to live such repressive lives…? Even if you study hard, get good grades, go to a good college, get a good job and make a ton of money, your happiness isn't guaranteed. I feel so frustrated by such narrow-minded values. There's something so wrong with studying for grades. This kind of "studying"—cramming before exams and then forgetting everything—is meaningless. Korean universities these days seem to be about taking classes that offer easier grades. There's no freedom to study what you really want to learn. I desperately wish Koreans could study in a freer environment.

~

I had never struggled with my weight before. In the US, I was naturally active in my daily life, from swimming and cheerleading to trampolining and dancing. My friends and I would talk about dieting and having a thigh gap, but I had a healthy relationship with food. Then, a few weeks into my new life at Myongji, I started putting on weight. It could have been the chocolate bars from the school store, the sudden lack of exercise or just puberty and hormones. One day I went to the bathroom after a big meal and shoved my index finger down my throat. I gagged as all the blood rushed to my face and my eyes became bloated and watery. A little harder. It felt good to rid myself of all the food. The finger went down more and more frequently, and the food came up more and more easily. I didn't even need to shove a finger. My reflex stepped in if I just leaned over the toilet. It became so easy that I could puke after eating an ice cream. Sometimes I could feel the food coming up even when I was just leaning over the top bunk in my dorm room.

I lost 7 kilos in two weeks and felt happy to be thin. Who knew weight loss could be so easy? I knew it was unsustainable, but I never meant to do it for a long time.

When I stopped vomiting every meal, I yo-yoed fast—I still have the stretch marks on my thighs. So, whenever I had a big meal, I would still vomit, taking care no one could see or hear me in the communal toilets.

Looking back, I don't think I was vomiting purely to lose weight. It was something I was doing for control. I hated school. I hated my straitlaced teachers and the stupid superintendents. The lessons were a waste of time, I wasn't learning anything, and I was at the bottom of my class. Nothing about the school was working for me.

I begged my mom, "Can you please take me out of this school? Can't I be homeschooled? What about an international school? What if I went to one of those liberal alternative schools?" (Realistically, international schools were prohibitively expensive. They were only affordable when we were abroad and receiving government aid.)

"We can't expect you to be like the other Korean kids," she said. I think my mom was reminding herself, reassuring herself, as much as she was trying to be understanding of me. It's true: contrary to the all-A expectations when I was abroad, I was never scolded for my grades in Korea.

My mom was no "study, study, study" tiger mom. She had been a model student herself, the class president all three years of high school, but she also valued life outside of the classroom. When I was in second grade, my mom took me and my brother out of school one day to go to Caribbean Bay, a gigantic water park. "*Miss a day of school!*" the other moms would have balked. But we had the best time, hopping from ride to ride without once having to queue. I didn't get my perfect attendance award that year, but who cared?

"I've always been so proud of how well you adapted in each country," my mom continued. "It'll be the same here. Just give it some time."

No, no, no. She clearly didn't understand. "Can you *please* put me back into your womb?" I said. It sounds silly, but I truly meant it. I'd visualize myself curling up in her womb, nice and snug, back to oblivion, just the way it was before I was born.

If school days really were the best days of our lives, what was the point of life?

17

Before the first day of school, there was an orientation week at an activities park. I realize how awfully superior this will sound, but I remember being appalled by what everyone was wearing and couldn't imagine being friends with any of them. They were exactly the kind of people I would have avoided at all costs in the US, not only because they were Asian but because they just looked so nerdy. But I knew I had no choice. I would need to make friends with some of them.

It was a common interest in boys that drew me, Sujin, Hyunah and Areum together and set us apart from the rest of our class. Areum was considered one of the prettiest girls. Even before school started, people were talking about the selfies she had posted on Cyworld, the Korean Myspace, with her lips pursed, peace sign pressed against her small face. "She's not as pretty in real life. It's all Photoshop," girls whispered, but she was popular with the boys. People compared me with Areum. I was apparently considered one of the pretty girls too. They said my face was small, which was bizarre because my big face had been a complex for me in America. I was used to seeing my face as big and flat, different from everyone else.

At the orientation, there was a concert organized by the gosam students and we were debating who the cutest boy was. The consensus seemed to be this tall, handsome guy who was the lead singer of his little band, though the girls were disappointed when rumors spread that he had a stunning girlfriend in his year. I set my eyes on another gosam who had come to welcome the newbies. He had a buzz cut, wore black glasses and was in no way good-looking but he was a charismatic speaker. With some prodding from my new friends, I accosted Buzz Cut and got his number.

After exchanging some texts, we started dating. In between breaks, I would visit his classroom and chat by the door, then scramble back to my floor when the bell rang. My classmates murmured when Buzz Cut came to visit me. Occasionally we had lunch together in the canteen, though it only invited the whole school to gossip. In the evenings, we met on the staircase or on the rooftop of the dormitory where we weren't allowed but went anyway.

It was big news, a first year and a gosam together, almost straight after school starting. To me, the whole concept of seniority among students was outlandish. I learned that students in the years above us were called *sunbae*. They were to be addressed with honorific titles and in the polite form. We had to *bow* to them. I understood bowing to teachers and adults but couldn't get my head around bowing to another student. I felt smug that I could do away with the bowing and use the informal form with Buzz Cut because I was dating him.

One night, maybe one or two in the morning, he texted: "Now." Heart racing, I tiptoed out of my room, down two flights of stairs to the boys' floor, taking care not to be caught on the CCTVs installed in the corridors. I gently pressed on the door handle and peeked in. He beckoned from the top left bunk. I tiptoed in, trying not to wake his roommates. We kissed and cuddled, and then he unsnapped my bra and touched my breasts. I stayed for another few hours, unable to fall sleep on the tiny mattress, then crept back to my room before everyone woke up.

The next day I realized I had left my bra in his room. How could I be so stupid? He returned it to me on the staircase that evening and reassured me that he hadn't told anyone. Unsurprisingly, rumors spread that I had slept with him. And rumors spread like wildfire at a boarding school. Standing in the canteen line, I could feel the stares and hear the whispers. It may as well have been shouted into a megaphone.

Within the first few months of school, I had managed to get myself a reputation. Everyone in the school knew me and for the wrong reasons. We broke up and he, of course, was not slut-shamed in the same way. I didn't do myself any favors. Girls who had lived abroad, who were Westernized and Americanized, were said to have had "a taste of American water." They were perceived to be easy. Instead of resisting that stereotype, I lived up to it. For me, it was meant to be fun. Wasn't it normal to fool around with boys at this age? I wish I'd known better.

～

My best friend Sujin was an attractive, well-rounded girl. She had been top of her class and the student body president in middle school but was also into boys and looking nice. Sujin was soon in a relationship with one of the class 3 boys, whom she proudly described as being "well known" in the cool circles. Like all cool boys, Dongho smoked, which Sujin made a point of worrying about. Their relationship exhibited all the teenage insecurities, with Sujin constantly asking me if I thought he really liked her. She'd tell me how much she liked him, then straight afterwards ask me if she should get back with an ex she was texting. But then she would tell me how sweet it was that Dongho had picked up on a subtle change of tone in her texts.

Sujin was determined to make her relationship last until "two-two." Koreans, I learned, celebrated everything from their first twenty-two days as a couple (hence two-two), then fifty days, a hundred days, two hundred days, three hundred days, and only then their anniversary. Sujin had already plotted the gifts for each occasion—she wanted to get couples' rings with Dongho on their fiftieth day.

I was soon set up with Dongho's best friend Minjoon, who turned out to be an expert texter. During class, I would text him under my desk on my Nokia slide phone, responding not so fast that it looked like I was waiting but speedily enough to keep the momentum going. I consulted Sujin on the tone of my messages and fawned over how cute and romantic he was.

Sujin dreamed of all the things we could do together. After midterms, we'll go on a double date to a theme park. We'll make it a competition, see which couple can go on more rides. Then we'll stay late for the night festival and laser show.

One morning, Hyunah said to me, "Hey, are you guys just not going to study? You and Sujin are so distracted."

Sure, Hyunah had the highest SAT score in our class, but who was she to say? I told Sujin about this, and she was annoyed too. Sujin and I had a couple's diary, which we passed back and forth several times a day. She listed all the reasons Hyunah was annoying:

Maybe I'm jealous but the way she's been making herself up lately, I can't stand to look at her. The way she says, "Come on, guys, let's quieten down," in class. Who does she think she is? That's the teacher's job. Is she feeling cocky because she's become friendly with [a senior boy]? The way she's trying so hard to get close to the class 9 boys. It pisses me off so much I might just make a move first.

I chimed in:

Yeah, it gets on my nerves when I see Hyunah trying so hard to be friendly with the class 9 boys. Maybe I'm jealous too. She's not that pretty, but she's skinny and she can look nice when she tries.

Unfortunately, it was true that Sujin's grades were slipping. She may have successfully juggled studying and boys in middle school, but that was less manageable at a wehgo.

≈

On Wednesdays, we could get a pass to go outside for a valid reason, though what counted as a valid reason was at the discretion of our insufferable homeroom teacher. The class 9 boys would find it much easier to get her approval. Even when we failed to get a pass, Sujin and I escaped as often as we could. We would crawl under the chain-link fence at the far side of the school grounds, then sprint down the hill. Sometimes we'd stay in the area, sometimes we'd take the bus to the nearest town. At first, it was thrilling and fun; later, we just wanted to slip out and slip back in without being noticed.

Once, on my way to join some friends at karaoke, I bumped into my gym teacher who was leaving the PC room next to it. *Fuck, what was he even doing there?* I bowed, quickly trying to hide the can of beer in my hands, but he just gave me a knowing smile and looked away. As I slipped into the karaoke room, I saw he was joined by some other teachers who I know wouldn't have been nearly as lenient. I always liked this gym teacher.

Sujin went out even more than I did, often with her boyfriend. In our couple's diary, I warned her to lie low as a group of boys in another class had just been busted:

> *Hey, I'm really saying this for your sake. Please stop breaking out. I know you got a pass this time, but you would've gotten in trouble if you'd been caught. I really think you'd get expelled if you got caught now, even if to set an example for the other kids. You can go out again when the rules relax a bit. I know it's not my place to be telling you what to do. I'm just worried something will happen.*

While Sujin didn't get annoyed with me, or at least she didn't show it, Hyunah must have said something to her too. Sujin wrote back:

I know, I had to go out today because I was going crazy. I had to buy something too. Anyway, why is Hyunah pretending to care when we don't even talk? It's so fake. What does she care whether I go out or not? Does my going out and coming back late impact her life in any way? She should mind her own business if she has the time to be nosing around. What's the point in saying this anyway...

Not long after that, Sujin said she had something to tell me. She was transferring to another school, and the next day would be her last. I hadn't seen that coming at all. I felt so blindsided that Sujin, my closest inmate, was bailing on me.

Just days earlier, Areum had left the school to move to the US. But Sujin? I had always been the one to leave. Is this what it was like to be left behind? I'd told Sujin that she was one of three true friends I'd ever had, alongside Mary and Julia.

"You're seriously leaving me for Lego hair?" I protested. Sujin was transferring to a girls' school that required her hair to be no longer than "two centimeters below her ears." I couldn't believe Sujin, who loved putting extensions in her hair, would accept this new haircut. Maybe it was her mom's doing. But this was just after the summer break—she must have been contemplating the transfer for some time. I felt so betrayed she hadn't even consulted me. I felt even more betrayed when it became obvious she wanted to spend her last night at Myongji with her boyfriend, whom she'd barely made it to two-two with; she and I had been friends from the very start.

~

After Sujin left, I thought harder about whether I should transfer too or drop out and earn a high school diploma. How could I possibly survive school now? It had been bad enough as it was.

I wished my mom would do what all the other moms of maladjusted kids were doing. I texted and called her, begging her to get me out of there. Instead, she made prison visits during the week, and we sat in her car in the parking lot. She would bring me her signature cheesecake, which she intended for me to share with my friends (what friends?), but I devoured in one sitting.

I recently broached this topic again with my mom. "You know, I really wish you'd listened to me back then."

"What do you mean?" she said.

"Taken me out of school."

Her face went blank, like she didn't understand.

"I clearly wasn't doing well," I added, flustered that a further explanation was even required.

She opened her mouth to speak, then hesitated. After a long pause, she finally said, "I would do it exactly the same if we were to turn back time."

I hadn't expected her to respond this way, to defend herself. "Why is it so difficult for you to admit that it was wrong? I'm telling you now"—my voice was rising—"as an adult, that that school did so much damage to me. We can't change the past. I just wish you'd acknowledge that that school was wrong for me. Why is it so difficult for you to say this?"

"What was I meant to do? Take you out of school? God forbid, home-school you? You don't really think that, do you?"

I did, as a matter of fact. "You know what? Never mind, forget I said anything. There's no point having this conversation with you."

Even after all these years, I was fuming. My mom is a reasonable person, so I couldn't understand why she was so adamant on this point. It wouldn't change my view of what a great mom she was and is, how much she loved and loves me, how she was only doing her best. How could she still not see where I was coming from?

Part of me wishes I could let it go. It benefits no one, certainly not me, to stay so resentful, but I just can't seem to, at least not yet. In fact, as I was writing these chapters, I had a variation of the same dream three nights in a row. I am back at this school, pleading with my mom and teachers to take me out, telling them that I have already been to university, that I have a job. But no one listens. People walk past me. I am invisible.

❧

With no best friend to rely on, I started hanging out with some girls from the other classes. One evening, a bunch of us from across the year planned a major escape. We had a great time at karaoke but got caught on the way back in.

The next morning, the school tannoy read out all the offenders starting from class 1, class 2, class 3, then "Lena Lee from class 4," then on and on. Everyone to report to the principal's office.

I'd already been suspended once before. That time, it was with a few boys, and we had to sit in the library all day, like in *The Breakfast Club*. This time, all of us were sent home for a week. My mom came to pick me up, and we drove home in silence.

The other girls didn't speak to me when we returned to school. It felt like I was being blamed for their suspension, as if I was the ringleader. Maybe I was, I don't know.

~

At the start of the second year, a new girl joined my class. Reeon was born in Ohio but had also moved around a lot and had just moved from Massachusetts. I hadn't had a close friend since Sujin left, so was happy to befriend her. I knew we would get on well. Even our names sounded similar. They both started with "Iri"—in Korean, my full name is pronounced Irina as Lee is pronounced "E" and your surname comes first—and people referred to us as the "Iri" pair.

Like me, Reeon struggled with her studies. Her passions were art and film, which there was no place for at this school. I showed her the ropes at Myongji and less than a month after she arrived, we got caught during one of our escapes and were suspended for one week. My third suspension. It was my mom's birthday then. While she was out, I blew two dozen balloons to surprise her. It was my way of saying sorry.

After three suspensions, it was finally determined that I was not suited to boarding school life and got a day student card. It was meant to be a punishment to be kicked out, but it's what I'd wished for all along. I had to commute an hour and twenty minutes each way, taking two subway lines and a bus. I still had to stay for my evening classes, so it was late and tiring by the time I got home, but it was still better than prison life.

Then, Reeon was taken out of school.

There was a clear pattern. It was rare for students to leave wehgo given how competitive admissions were, but the curse of befriending me was reason enough. The school moms (and some dads) were hysterical about everything and regarded me as the bad apple who would corrupt their faultless children. I knew they were generally quick to sneer and pass judgment and can only imagine the humiliation my mom suffered at parents' evenings.

That's what I find most upsetting, that my misbehavior was not seen as youthful transgressions but as if I was some truly bad, morally corrupt person. As if I was a lost cause.

18

In early 2008, my parents started discussing what to do with me. We were coming up to three years in Korea and it would soon be time for my dad's next international posting. I was a gosam, the fateful year that would determine the rest of my life. My grades were abysmal, and I hated school, but I had less than a year left. I could remain at the boarding school and stay with my grandma on weekends. Did it make sense to take me to a new school in a new country at this point? It was a big risk. My parents didn't even know where the next assignment would be. We only ever found out the destination when the official appointment was made two to three months before. It wasn't ideal for planning. As for me, I just wanted to get out. Leave the school, leave Korea. Anything but here.

But as fate would have it, I fell in love just around this time. It was with a boy from class 9—the one called *hyung*—whom I'd shared a classroom with for two years. He wasn't particularly tall, athletic, smart or handsome. In fact, he was only a few inches taller than me and weighed even less than me. I'm not sure how it started, who made the first move, but I think it was during the winter break before gosam. We somehow ended up at karaoke together, him and his friend and me and my friend. He would sing a kind of Korean "My Sharona" but sing it as "My Lena"—painfully out of tune.

From there, it all happened fast. Maybe it was a familiarity, a fondness grown over time, though that made things awkward too. By virtue of him being in class 9, we were meant to be sworn enemies. I didn't even know what to call him. I'd only ever called him by his full name—Lee Yoonhak. But then he started calling me by my first name only ("Lena-ya"), then we progressed to calling each other "*jagi*" or sweetheart. Once we got over the initial cringe, it felt natural soon enough. It also became too obvious to bother being discreet at school. Our classmates started noticing us holding hands. All our teachers found out too, but we didn't care. Even though we'd only been together a few months, it felt so comfortable and familiar, like we'd always been together.

Then the official appointment was made: Paris. In some ways, it felt like I'd been granted early release from my three-year sentence. I'd never been to Europe and tried to imagine what life might be like there. At the same time, I dreaded having to tell Yoonhak. But he saw what was coming. We sat inside a playhouse after school one day and he cried and he cried. I'd never seen a boy cry like that. I took off the purple sweater I was wearing so we could wipe our tears and blow our noses on it. His vulnerability made me feel more protective of him, love him even more.

I was torn. Was it too late to change my mind about Paris? How could I have known I would fall in love? I didn't even know what love would feel like.

But I knew it was too late. Yoonhak and I were both realistic and knew a long-distance relationship would never work. Even if I stayed at Myongji, we would probably end up in different universities in different countries. Still, it felt devastating, the fact that our relationship was going to be terminated by an uncontrollable external factor just as it was beginning.

With less than a month left, we would have to make the most of our time together, at school, after school, on weekends. We wouldn't get to do all the things other Korean couples do, like getting matching rings and celebrating our hundredth day together.

~

"Are you sure you want to do this?" Yoonhak asked. We were lying on a bed-sized leather couch in a small, dark room as some random movie played on the screen.

"Yes," I said. "Do you know how to do it?"

"I've seen it plenty of times," he said, trying to lighten the mood.

"Gross!"

Nervously, we took off our clothes. Then he positioned himself on top of me.

"Is it okay?" he asked.

It was, and it wasn't. This wasn't how I had wanted to do it, but time wasn't on our side. It was now or never.

~

A few days later was our last day together. We bought matching silver keyrings, the shape of a little girl with a pink rhinestone and a boy with a blue rhinestone. We took sticker photos, me cuddling into his chest, his arm wrapped around me, and scribbled things like "*jagi*" and "us in ten years."

Even though we were being separated now, I felt hopeful that maybe it could work out one day. I told him I wanted to marry him. I wanted to be with him forever. We might have to go our separate ways now, and we'll date other people, but you never knew with these things. Maybe we'll find our way back to each other.

I still have the receipt from the coffee shop we went to on our last evening together. It's faded now but you can make out the stamp: one iced caramel macchiato ordered 2008/05/25 20:36. It's definitely his order—he could consume all the calories in the world and still be stick thin, which I hated him for.

We listed on a piece of paper thirty things we wanted to do together, things we didn't have the time for now, then ripped the paper in half and each kept a piece. I have promises 7 to 11 and 25 to 30. I don't know what was on his half—he probably threw it away—but mine say we'd go to a jjimjilbang together, we'd scream from the top of a mountain, and finally number 30: we'd stay in touch forever.

We knew it wasn't going to be easy. "What should I do if I still want to hug you and kiss you when we meet again?" he said. "Please don't scream 'pervert' and run away if I do that." I couldn't imagine that.

We said our final goodbye at a bus stop. As I waved to him sitting in the back of the bus, there was a sharp pain in my heart. Until then I'd thought "heartbreak" was a metaphor.

The next day I went to the airport with my parents. Slumped in a window seat, I texted him until the last moment, even as the plane was taking off. As the tears coursed down my cheeks, I vowed to never forget this feeling, that I would not look back at this as the time I was only sixteen and thought I was in love.

I still have the last letter he wrote me. I read it recently and cried just as I had back then:

P.S. It's funny writing a postscript like this. You know that "I love you" thing... It makes me so nervous saying that to you. So nervous and cautious... It makes my heart hurt so much... As if my heart is turning into mush. And it scares me... I don't want to say goodbye, but I don't think there is another way. But we're not saying goodbye because we no longer like each other and the fact that we'll at least meet again somewhat consoles me. I love you a lot...

19

"Lena, have you heard of Haussmann?" my dad asked in an upbeat tone as he drove me and my mom around Paris. "He's the man who transformed Paris into the city it is today." My dad spoke with pride as if he'd commissioned the work himself. It was my first time in Europe, and he liked acting the tour guide—his first trip abroad had been to France in 1983, when he was twenty-five.

Heartbroken, I feigned indifference. But as much as I refused to be impressed, I couldn't help admiring the historic monuments, the luscious gardens, the cobbled boulevards, the magnificent bridges. The streetlights looked like something out of *Beauty and the Beast*. The Eiffel Tower was right in front of us. This was *Paris*. And we weren't tourists; we were there to live. It felt surreal that this was our new reality.

Our new home was a three-bedroom apartment in an Haussmann building with cream-colored stone façades and two imposing wooden doors. It was located centrally in the eighth arrondissement, only a few minutes' walk from the Champs-Élysées. My parents and I (my brother was still at university in Korea) would go on many long walks up to Montmartre or along the Seine to Notre Dame or on an evening stroll to the Élysée Palace, where President Sarkozy lived. Jjanga always came with us, and the French would tease us for putting a leash on *"une petite souris"*—a little mouse. Thankfully, Jjanga only "spoke" Korean.

In many ways, the French seemed to live up to their stereotypes. They really did like their baguettes, fromage and red wine. True to their motto—*liberté, égalité, fraternité*— they regularly took to the streets (at the time, students were demonstrating against Sarkozy's university reforms). They seemed to enjoy life, committed to their thirty-five-hour work week, sipping an espresso or a glass of wine over their leisurely lunch breaks on terraces. They were fashionable: dressed in deceptively simple outfits, Parisian women seemed to pull off an air of effortless elegance about them.

Based on first impressions, however, the French were also rude. Not long after we arrived, while on a walk near the Eiffel Tower, my mom and I were stopped at a traffic light, facing a swarm of people also waiting to cross the road. When the light switched, I bumped into a man. *"Regarde!"* he shouted, scowling at me. The way he coughed up the "R" sound, I thought he was drawing up phlegm to spit on me. Were all French people like that? Was it because I was Asian? I felt a lump in my throat and wanted to return to Korea so badly in that moment.

My heart still ached. I knew from experience I would make new friends, but this felt different. I worried if I would ever get over my heartbreak. "I really can't do this. I want to go back," I told my mom tearfully, but she only gave me a sympathetic look.

137

My new school looked nothing like my previous schools. In fact, it didn't even look like a school. It was hidden behind a white brick wall on a nondescript one-way street lined by residential apartments. There was no sign except for a "70" written on top of a narrow door. My parents and I double-checked the address and rang the buzzer.

The receptionist brought us to meet Madame Dupont, the *Directrice Générale Adjointe*, head of admissions, a squat woman in her fifties, with short, bleached hair and a flushed face. *Bonjour, bonjour*, my dad led the greetings on our behalf, then before Madame Dupont could ask anything, he launched into an impassioned monologue. Even though I couldn't understand what he was saying, I could tell he was putting on every charm and Madame Dupont laughed at all his jokes. I was very impressed. I knew my dad had majored in French at university, but I had never seen him speak the language.

Thanks to my dad's stellar performance, I was accepted to start in September. What I hadn't understood from his conversation with Madame Dupont was that my classes would be taught in both English and French, and I had better be up to scratch in three months' time. Unlike other embassy kids who attended the international or American school, my parents had decided on a bilingual school for me so I could have the most authentic French experience short of throwing me into a local *lycée*.

There was no way I was going to become fluent in such a short period, but I was game. I took an intensive language course with a motley group of adults from around the world.

We weren't allowed to speak any English, so our teacher, whose bouncy curls and four-inch wedge heels I remember, would gesticulate wildly to get her point across, sometimes to comic effect. It felt like playing charades.

I loved learning French. I would listen to the radio and marvel at the sounds, occasionally snickering at the way they said "shampweng" for shampoo or "wee-fee" for Wi-Fi. I would practice on my mom what I'd learned on my course, sometimes improvising and no doubt teaching her some nonsense along the way. I wanted to practice my elementary French in shops and restaurants, but the locals would reply impatiently in English to prove that their broken English was at least better than my broken French. It sounds ridiculous now, but I was surprised how little English the French spoke. I'd assumed all white people spoke decent English. In time, I gained the confidence to persist in French even in the face of rude waiters, especially once I learned they were not necessarily being racist per se.

My parents and I would compare our levels of competency in French. My mom had no formal training but had picked up some French in Rwanda nearly two decades earlier. She'd been taught informally by a Canadian expat, though a French friend privately advised her against picking up a silly Quebecois accent. While I no longer remembered anything, I had taken some French classes back in Malaysia and America and was catching up fast. My dad would ask me leading questions to slyly check that he still had the lead in French grammar, his strong suit. My mom had the best pronunciation by far—she had an ear for languages and was good at mimicking the sounds and cadence of a native speaker—which irked my dad to no end as his accent could not be improved with practice. He hated having to ask for "*du beurre*" (butter) at restaurants. Even polite French waiters struggled to understand him until my mom whispered "*beurre*" under her breath and the waiter would exclaim, "*Ah, beurre! Excusez-moi, monsieur.*" My accent was neither Korean nor American. I struggled with the "R" sound, as in *rue* (street), *ouvrir* (to open) and *sourire* (to smile)—much like my dad struggling with his Rs in English.

~

After a summer of intensive French lessons, I started the International Baccalaureate, a two-year diploma program. I was being "held back" in a sense as I would have graduated in a semester in Korea, but it was an opportunity to start afresh, both academically and socially, to learn a new language and experience a new country and continent.

So much for the fresh start, I was late on my first day. Well, I had arrived at the school an hour and a half early and decided to wait at a nearby café. Sitting by the window, I watched the throngs of mostly white teenagers hanging out on the sidewalk, some coolly leaning against the railing. I examined them closely. They greeted each other with kisses on the cheek, once on the right, once on the left, holding their cigarettes out of the way. It looked like they were catching up on their summer vacations. I contemplated my outfit—a yellow round neck sweater from Zara, dark skinny jeans and a pair of leather flats, all of which I'd bought that summer—and tried to assess whether I had dressed appropriately.

As 3 p.m. approached, the kids continued to chatter away, the boys playfully jostling each other. I decided to join them outside, but as I rose, all the blood in my body rushed to my head, my knees almost buckling. It felt like everyone was staring at me. I finally mustered the courage to tap a cigarette-wielding kid on the shoulder and ask why everyone was still hanging around. It turned out I was waiting with the wrong group of people. These were the *terminale*, or seniors. I should have been with the *premières* who were already in the *amphithéâtre*, in another building on the other side of the street.

"There you are, Lena!" Ms. Burchill hollered in her deep, husky voice when I opened the door and peeped in. Everyone turned around to inspect the latecomer.

"Hi, sorry!" I said, out of breath. I found an empty seat at the back and scanned the room. There were nearly fifty of us, a mix of ethnicities. I could see a handful of Koreans who unsurprisingly sat together. I knew I was not the only new kid, but I still hated being *a* new kid. I didn't know if I could do this yet again. Paris was my opportunity to "reinvent" myself, which I desperately wanted to do after Korea, but I no longer knew who I was or even wanted to be.

I hoped someone would talk to me. One girl turned around and asked if I had a pair of scissors. Other than that, no one spoke to me that day. It seemed first days got harder each time.

20

My class timetable was presented as if we were in the
military—16h00 rather than 4 p.m.—but my days were far
from regimented. During free periods, I would sometimes
go window shopping in the nearby Commerce area, as if it
were all part of the school grounds. Sometimes I took the
Métro home to have lunch with my mom before returning to
school for my afternoon classes. It was hard to believe that
only months earlier, I had been fenced inside a prison-like
environment where the only way to get out was to break out.

On the first day of class, our no-nonsense English
teacher with a thick mustache asked, "Who's actually read
the book?" Mr. Thompson looked around, perched on
top of his desk. We were supposed to have read *Heart of
Darkness* as our summer assignment, but I scrolled through
the summary on SparkNotes instead after the nautical
jargon tripped me up from the first sentence—what was a
"yawl"? From the way they avoided his gaze, I gathered my
classmates had not read the book either. We would spend
the first trimester mastering this one little book, reading out
passages, repeating sentences to hear the rhythm, the rhythm
of the tides. I scribbled all over it, linking paragraphs with

arrows and circling symbolic words like "grass" and "snake."

Mr. Thompson would call on us to share our views. There was no right answer, no multiple-choice question telling us what the correct interpretation was. Some of my peers' responses seemed far-fetched, but Mr. Thompson never put anyone down. Everyone was entitled to their view. At first, I was embarrassed to say anything, but with his encouragement, my confidence grew. Importantly, I was discovering the joys of reading.

Unlike my teachers in Korea, Mr. Thompson treated us like adults. He was a firm atheist and didn't hide it, casually likening Jesus to Jove. "OUR DEITIES ARE INVENTED," my notes say. When we studied the poem "Digging" by Seamus Heaney, he told us the pen, the spade, the gun, the rhythmic digging, they were all phallic imagery. I wondered at first if he was maybe being a little overzealous, but I soon learned to identify such sexual allusions myself. Any kind of sniggering or looks exchanged during class did not go down well.

Math was taught in French by the lovely Madame Spanjaard, a veteran teacher in her sixties who was most respectful of her students, always addressing us as *vous*. (In French, students must *vouvoie* their teachers, but teachers tend to *tutoie* their students.) I understood most of her class, though I had to strain my ears when it came to numbers, like *quatre-vingt-dix* ((4x20) +10) for ninety, thanks to their erratic vigesimal system. Confusingly, a thousand is *mille*, a million is *million* and a billion is *milliard*. And because I learned my times table back in Korea, I still do all my basic calculations in Korean. I also count in Korean, though unconsciously switch to English once a thousand separator is needed because for some reason, Koreans count in ten-thousands, rather than thousands, just to spice things up.

Higher-level math in the IB was challenging, but importantly, doable. Unlike in Korea, I knew I could do well if I tried, so I paid attention in class and found myself almost enjoying math. When Madame Spanjaard handed back our tests, everyone waited for me to get mine. Two boys were particularly competitive and wanted to beat me, though they rarely did.

Across subjects, my teachers were suddenly saying I was "excellent," "brilliant" and "*remarquable*." Our indomitable headmistress, Ms. Burchill, liked to point me out in front of the entire year as an exemplary student. It must have sounded like Lena this, Lena that.

I felt like a fraud. Had I really changed overnight? If only they knew what I'd been like in Korea.

~

I became friends with Lynn through English class. Lynn was from Cork, Ireland, and Mr. Thompson loved that, unlike the rest of us, she had heard of Joyce and Beckett and Seamus Heaney. Lynn's father was an Irish Army Officer, and she had recently moved to Paris too. I noticed she said "tanks" instead of thanks and "you-RAHY-nuhl" for urinal. She called cigarettes "fags," which sounded offensive to my American ear.

Lynn was pale and pretty with freckles and brown layered hair. Besides the fact that she was Irish, Lynn looked nothing like my friends in Korea. She wore heavy black eye makeup and tweezed her eyebrows thin. She had lean legs which she liked to show off in tight jeans or a short skirt, almost always black, paired with a leather jacket and boots, and always a "fag" snapped between her fingers.

Maybe it was our mutual foreigner and new kid status or the fact that neither of us spoke French well, but we quickly became friends. We would go over to each other's houses, and I remember she introduced me to bacon rashers with brown sauce at her place. We'd buy booze from the local "*arabe*" and get drunk on the Champ de Mars. At seventeen, we were too young to buy hard liquor but could legally drink wine and beer. One time Lynn and I went to Pigalle, the red-light district by the Moulin Rouge, and visited a strip club out of hours. We said we were looking for jobs and a lady showed us in through burgundy velvet curtains. She asked us about our experience and if we could come in for a trial. Lynn and I left giggling, wondering how they never once asked us our age. It reminded me of my mischievous days in America.

I smoked weed for the first time with Lynn and two boys from my school. I was curious to know what it felt like to get high. But I didn't feel anything, probably because I coughed more than I inhaled. After drinking some Malibu, we went to a house party. The next thing I knew, I was in an emergency room with a drip in my left arm. Apparently, I had passed out. My parents were there, looking concerned but not mad. I wasn't sure how they would react if I told them what I'd taken—in Korea, cannabis is as taboo as, say, cocaine is in the West—but amazingly, they remained calm. I think more than anything, my mom was just glad that I had made new friends.

21

If I worked hard and played hard during my first year in Paris, things changed, or maybe I changed, in *terminale*. Because I had been held back a year for the IB, my friends at wehgo were going off to college when I started my senior year. A few made it to Ivy League schools like Cornell and Columbia, places I wouldn't have stood a chance at in Korea but which now seemed within reach. I didn't want to waste this opportunity.

As I excelled academically, some classmates started asking me for my homework. One boy wasn't even in the same class but asked me for help with his math homework. In return, he said he would teach me French. Kareem was one of the cool kids. He was of Tunisian origin and looked like Aladdin with his long, wavy hair, though he dressed very Parisian with his smart suede shoes. As agreed, during free periods, I helped Kareem with his math homework and he taught me *verlan*, or French slang where the syllables in a word are inverted (for instance, *femme* becomes *meuf*, *français* becomes *céfran*). I noticed one day the pendant on his gold necklace, which was usually hidden under his sweater, was an Islamic crescent and so I asked if he was

Muslim. He was coy about it, so I didn't probe further. I later learned that Kareem read the Quran and went to Islamic school on Saturdays. He reminded me of myself in the US. In private, Kareem would flirt with me, and I would flirt back, but when we saw each other in the corridors or he was with his friends, he would ignore me. I felt reduced to the Asian stereotype I had avoided becoming in the US: the one they only speak to for homework.

Not long before, a nice American boy who was a close friend of Kareem had asked me out to the movies. He was cute and I liked him, but I wasn't sure if it was a date. We ended up watching a French comedy, which was awkward because I couldn't understand much. When we said goodbye, straight after the movie, I wasn't sure if he would try to kiss me; we did the "*bise*" instead. The entire time, I couldn't stop wondering if this was a prank, if his friends had set him up. (I used to call Yoonhak when I first moved to Paris but with the time difference and cost—this was before smartphones—I had to stop. Also, my feelings for him faded over time, much the way hiccups stop without you even noticing.)

I never fitted in at this school. I realized it was the kind where the French president sent his children, where they had recognizable surnames and spent summer holidays in Saint-Tropez, where even the boys wore Gucci trainers. (My parents could afford the fees thanks to the government subsidy.) It reminded me of my middle school in America, the obsession with money and social status, though I had changed by this time. I didn't care about those things anymore. I became standoffish and untrusting, suspecting everyone had a hidden motive or was laughing at my expense.

Lynn and I grew apart too. There wasn't a fight or anything; we just drifted. As I became more focused on my academics, Lynn seemed unbothered by it all, even though her sister who was in the year above us—they were so-called "Irish twins"—had just been accepted at Harvard. If anything, that seemed to put her off college even more. Maybe it was sour grapes. Lynn did alright at school, but art was more her thing. I also never hung around when Lynn was taking her "fag breaks" in between classes. I hated the cigarette smoke. Many of the cool kids, however, smoked, and once she became friendly with them, she started ignoring me.

I decided I didn't need friends. With less than a year left, it was far more important that I get into a good university. I wasn't going to see any of these people again anyway. I had had enough of trying to fit in.

~

As my social life disintegrated during my second year in Paris, I found myself playing the piano more. Before we moved, my dad had tried to talk me out of shipping my Yamaha halfway around the world, especially when I barely practiced. Although I'd taken continuous lessons since I was five, it was never as a serious student. My mom was well aware of the total lack of musical talent in our family and just wanted me to have an instrument I would enjoy. She had tried the violin on my brother, a traumatic experience for both.

My piano was indeed an unwieldy piece of furniture to maneuver up three flights of stairs in our apartment building, which only had a miniature elevator, but I was glad we'd brought it. Until then, I'd only practiced when I had to. In Paris, I started playing because I wanted to. It could be a familiar sonatina or a pop song ("I Want It That Way" by the Backstreet Boys was a favorite), or the challenge of sight-reading and mastering a piece. I would sometimes play for hours in my room.

Jjanga comforted me too. I always thought of her as a sister, and not a pet. If I teased her too much, she would go find my mom and "tell on" me, just like a sibling would, though by growling and barking at me. She'd be spurred on by mom saying, "Poor Jjanga, was Lena mean to you?" Sometimes I put her under my shirt and she would pop her head out my neckline, the two of us looking like a two-headed creature. She loved to lie on my bed, though too small to jump up herself, she would "ask" me to pick her up. There were times I cried in bed with her and she would look at me so intently, as if she understood me. Jjanga had been one of the few continuities in my life. Which country had she enjoyed living in the most: Korea, Malaysia, America, France? It couldn't have been easy, even for her.

My alienation from school also brought me closer to my mom. It was already so much easier no longer having to beg her to take me out of boarding school. She was more like a friend now and we would go shopping together—our tastes in fashion had converged since the US and I was as excited about sales as she was. We talked a lot too, though I never told her what I was really going through at school.

Things were still awkward with my dad. In the mornings, he drove me to school on his way to the embassy. He'd always leave the house five minutes before me so he could collect the car and park it right outside for me. As in the past, we didn't speak much on these journeys. Sometimes we listened to the news on the radio. I would only mutter a "*ddeng-kyoo*" (Korean pronunciation of "thank you") or a "*merci*" before I got out. Once, a classmate saw me being dropped off in our black Mercedes—the embassy car—and asked if my dad was my driver. I guess it could have looked like that.

For vacations, we went on road trips around the country, from Normandy and Brittany to the Champagne region and the castles along the Loire Valley. My dad always drove, my mom gave directions, and I sat in the back with Jjanga. Sometimes it got tense in the car, when my dad complained about the quality of my mom's navigation, for instance, but I have many good memories too.

~

That fall, with the support of my college counselor, I applied early to Yale. My grades were strong, my standardized test scores were near-perfect, and I could count on my teachers for strong recommendation letters. I was arguably the most promising candidate from my school.

A few months later, though, I found out that my early application to Yale had been deferred to the spring, while two of my peers, both of whom I felt were weaker candidates than me, had been accepted. One of them had "legacy." I cried so much that morning, I was late to school and showed up puffy-eyed halfway through English class. Everyone knew why I was late, and Mr. Thompson was most sympathetic.

In the end, I was rejected from Harvard and Yale and wait-listed at Princeton. Luckily, I had another offer. I'd only considered American colleges until my history teacher Mr. Bunch suggested I apply to Oxford, his alma mater, and somehow I passed the interviews. Still, my failure to get into Harvard, Yale or Princeton rankled as these were some of the few fully "need-blind" schools, meaning they provided financial aid even to international students. At Oxford, my parents would have to pay the full tuition fee.

What bothered me even more was that kids at my school, many of whom were academically mediocre at best, were accepted to Brown, the prestigious hotel school at Cornell and the Wharton School of UPenn (two of them!). I hadn't even applied to these colleges but felt indignant all the same. It seemed that with the right background, money and legacy preferences, you could waltz into an Ivy League. To be clear, my anger is directed more at these elite institutions which continue to reward privilege over merit rather than the students who got into them. Of course, I have no doubt that my own privilege played a huge role in my getting into Oxford. But surely there were far more deserving candidates around the world.

~

In May 2010, I sat my final exams. By this point, I had an unconditional offer from Oxford but I was stressed all the same, as I'd been conditioned to be for every exam. My dad sent me some words of encouragement in his characteristic style:

I understand the school has high expectations of you and hope you get the best score ever and thus open a new chapter in the history of the school: 45 out of 45. That's fantastic, isn't it? I am confident you will surely live up to these high expectations.

Unfortunately, I didn't. Could I ever? But I got 44 out of 45 (I lost one mark in History), and was done with school, finally and forever.

When I left the US at fourteen, I was heartbroken to leave my best friends. When I left Korea at seventeen, I was heartbroken to leave my boyfriend. When I left Paris at nineteen, I felt nothing but excitement to start afresh, once again.

22

"Here's the Beehive," the student ambassador said, a little too cheerfully. After passing through beautiful stone archways and quadrangles that exuded history and tradition, my first-year accommodation was a building covered in Portland Stone, apparently meant to represent some kind of postwar modernist architecture. It was no more impressive inside. My room was hexagonal, hence the moniker, and the ceiling coned like a teepee. Besides a single bed on a metal frame, with a dingy brick-colored duvet cover that matched the curtains and carpet, there was a desk, a small fridge and a hand basin. There were separate taps for hot and cold water—the hot tap was too hot, and the cold tap too cold—and they were fixed on each side of the basin. I would learn to cup my hands briefly under the cold water before swinging around to the hot tap to achieve a sensible temperature.

One good thing about the Beehive, though, was that it was conveniently located just across the quad from the dining hall, where I would have most of my meals. As soon as they saw me coming for breakfast, the friendly chefs would pile my plate high with mushrooms—my favorite—before I even had a chance to say good morning. In the evenings, I enjoyed going to Formal Hall, where we ate heavily subsidized three-course meals in our formal gowns and stood for grace to be spoken in Latin before dinner—all part of the "Oxford experience," I would learn.

During freshers' week, which is British speak for college orientation, everyone asked each other what school they went to, what GCSEs and A-levels they took and compared how many A*s they got. It was all gibberish to me. "What's a GCSE?" I'd ask, interrupting the conversation and exposing my foreigner status. Here I was, an Asian girl with an American accent saying she'd come from a bilingual high school in Paris. ("Asian," I would learn, is used more commonly in the UK to describe South Asians than East Asians.) Even more confusingly, in between terms, I would go "home" to Norway where my dad was now the ambassador. People couldn't quite place me, and I felt like an outsider.

There were surprisingly many words and phrases that confused me even, or especially, during casual conversations. When someone was *fit*, it meant they were sexy, not athletic. *Pissed* meant drunk, not angry. Brits were *chuffed*, rather than pleased; *knackered*, rather than tired. Underwear were *pants*; pants were *trousers*. (Never say you don't wear pants!) They *popped* to the *loo*. They went to the *cinema* to watch a *film*. *Fancy a cuppa?* meant "Would you like a cup of tea?" When it came to food, it was *pudding* for dessert and *supper* for dinner. *Chips* were french fries; *crisps* were potato chips. Then the curse words: *blimey*, *bollocks*, *bloody*, *bugger*.

It was also the British manner of speech. On the one hand, nothing was ever good; it was "not bad." On the other hand, mundane things were suddenly brilliant, splendid and marvelous!

What I called Q-tips and Band-Aids were cotton swabs and plasters. A vacuum was a Hoover. Waterstones was their Barnes & Noble. I didn't know Waitrose from Aldi, or where the *Telegraph* and *Guardian* sat on the political spectrum. Passing references to popular TV shows such as *EastEnders* and *Strictly Come Dancing* were lost on me. I knew nothing of British politics or the royal family tree. I didn't know what a bank holiday or a pub crawl was. I didn't even know what the NHS was, and that everyone, including me, got free healthcare in the UK. I kept trying to pay every time I visited my GP.

~

I had never heard of the word "posh" until I came to Oxford and was largely oblivious to one of the most defining aspects of the British social scene—gauging accents and class—until I met Hannah during freshers' week. Hannah was from Bournemouth, on the southern coast of England, and had largely grown up with a single mom who was a care home nurse. She had gone to a local comprehensive school, where she was bullied for being too smart and hard-working. Hannah explained to me that "public schools" were, in fact, fee-paying private schools. I had not heard of Harrow or Westminster, Cheltenham or Wycombe Abbey, names to which others seemed to react with an instant knowing look.

I couldn't even distinguish between the different British accents, let alone an Irish, Australian or South African one.

Hannah was an evangelical Christian and was reading Theology (though she'd later change her course to History and Portuguese). She would tell me about her faith and how important it was to her. On Sundays, she went to this hip Brazilian church where they strummed gospel songs on the guitar, and I would tag along every now and again. Sometimes she invited me to talks around the university with titles like "Why is there suffering if there is a God?" not necessarily to convert me but to share a part of her world. I never found any of them convincing but would politely thank her for inviting me.

Even as a little girl, I never believed in God. Although my parents are non-believers—I'm not sure if they are agnostic or atheist—they subscribed to the notion of the Good Christian and sent me to church when I was seven or so in Korea. I remember going to an overnight camp once, and the priest was wailing about "yeh-soo-greece-doh" (it clicked only years later that this was Jesus Christ). The kids started crying for some reason. I was dumbfounded. I couldn't understand what this naked man nailed to a cross, someone who apparently died 2,000 years ago, had anything to do with me. I forced a yawn to squeeze a tear out. What confused me even more as a child was why so many adults believed in God.

Years later, Richard Dawkins gave words to my instincts and reaffirmed my views on God and religion. I had discovered Dawkins when I read *The Selfish Gene* as part of my Oxford interviews preparation. Then I devoured his other books on evolutionary theory, as well as *The God Delusion*.

I loved his writing, always so clear, witty and logical, even on a subject as complex and loaded as religion. I would watch YouTube videos of the young Richard Dawkins and think, *What a charismatic guy.* He was my intellectual crush, and possibly a bit more than that—I was taught by his ex-wife, also a renowned biologist, but pathetically couldn't help wondering in the lecture hall: *What did he see in her?* To believers, though, Dawkins was a militant atheist and a fundamentalist no better than those he was denouncing. So whenever Hannah came over to my room, I dumped my copy of *The God Delusion* in my drawer.

Hannah and I often discussed our essay topics for the week but the seemingly innocuous topic could turn awkward when mine was about evolution. I loved studying the behavior of chimpanzees, our closest cousins, but I knew Hannah found the proximity disturbing, if not false. I always worried about offending her. I couldn't relate to Hannah's essay topics on Matthew, Mark, Luke and John either, so we would find a way to politely change the subject. Her evangelicalism and my atheism never got in the way of our friendship.

~

My course, Human Sciences, allowed me to study our species from multiple perspectives, covering everything from anthropology to sociology, demography to ecology, genetics to evolution. I loved the breadth of my studies and drawing connections between the various disciplines. My favorite part was studying animal behavior, particularly that of primates, for the light it cast on human behavior.

For instance, if social relationships—hierarchy, alliances and friendships—were so integral to chimpanzee life, didn't that say something about our evolutionary need to belong? On a personal level, it seemed to explain my intense desire to fit in every time we moved to a new country. What I loved most about Oxford, though, was that studying wasn't a means to an end. I could read as many books and articles as I wanted on whatever I found interesting. There were endless routes for discovery.

Apart from attending some lectures and tutorials, it was up to me to manage my own time. I loved the autonomy and became obsessed with my routine. Surrounded by historic libraries like the Bodleian, one of the oldest libraries in Europe, I studied at the Starbucks on Cornmarket Street. I would leave early in the morning when it was still dark out and sometimes arrive before the store manager. Even though I would only order a filter coffee, which meant I could get unlimited refills and sit around all morning, I was never made to feel unwelcome. I had my usual seat upstairs against a wall (by a plug, importantly) where I would read my books and articles and write my essays. Even as the floor became busier and filled with tourists, everything else blurred out when I was in flow.

By the time I returned to my room in the mid-afternoon, soaked in the smell of coffee roast, my brain would be in overdrive. I needed some way to unwind but I didn't know how. This is when I started drinking by myself in my room, and my relationship with alcohol changed fundamentally. Before then, I would get smashed with my friends in America or during escapes at boarding school, but I hadn't felt the compulsive need to drink. Now I *needed* it to loosen up.

I knew it wasn't a socially acceptable hour to drink yet. Nor did I want to be sociable. I didn't like the self-consciousness of drinking with other people, having to keep up a front, making sure I didn't get too drunk, saying or doing anything I would regret or spending the next day trying to remember. If I'd started drinking in the US to get up to silly antics, now I drank to decompress, as something to take the edge off when my brain was all revved up from the day's studies.

I went through phases with my choice of tipple. I would drink strictly rosé for a few months, then for some reason (likely a bad hangover), move on to a new drink as if that meant I got a clean slate. When my room was just above the college bar, I brought up draught cider, though this phase didn't last long as cider gave me heartburn. Then I had my red wine phase and amaretto and coke phase. My all-time favorite was bubbly.

On a typical day, I drank somewhere between a bottle and two of wine. Occasionally I had days off. Looking back, I don't know how I woke up so early to read and write essays after consuming so much alcohol day in and day out, but somehow I managed. Even then, I knew I was drinking too much and not in the socially acceptable way, but then again didn't everyone get drunk at university?

~

At the end of each term, tutors submitted feedback on our performance, which was then read aloud by a head tutor, sometimes making for an entertaining read. One of my tutors, a PhD student I was not particularly impressed with, noted: "Scepticism sometimes lies beneath her inscrutable expression."

A tutor I held in the highest esteem was Alan Grafen, a former doctoral student of Richard Dawkins, my intellectual hero. I was hugely intimidated by Alan even before I met him, not least because he looked like the academic genius type. He had unkempt silver hair and a truly inscrutable expression. I felt like he could see things the rest of us couldn't. I did my best to prepare for his tutorials, taking extra care when citing his articles, and was no less intimidated by him by the end. I had no idea what he thought of me.

Alan wrote in my feedback—now please indulge me for a moment here—that I was "clearly an exceptional student, with few equals in [his] experience." I jumped up and down at this unexpectedly flattering report and emailed it to my parents.

My imagination went wild. Richard Dawkins himself had studied under Niko Tinbergen, the Nobel Prize-winning founder of modern ethology, or the study of animal behavior. So, I entertained—just for a moment—the possibility of a lineage from Tinbergen, Dawkins and Grafen to myself. Maybe I wasn't so bad. Contrary to the low-grade cattle that I was in Korea, maybe I had potential.

Then, on the last day of our second year, Hannah and I made a day trip to London before we broke off for the summer. We got back on a late-night train, drinking some rosé on the way. It was pouring when we arrived at Oxford station past midnight. While everyone was scrambling to catch a cab, I bumped into a Korean friend who, pointing at a cab that was driving away, said, "That was Richard Dawkins there."

"What?!" Without thinking, I started sprinting in that direction. When the cab slowed down, I rapped at the back door window as if I had an urgent message. The window pulled down and there he was: Richard Dawkins.

"What *is* it?" he snapped.

"Oh my god, I am such a fan," I said. *A fan? Seriously?* As if he was some pop star.

When it looked like I wasn't going away, he said, "Get in then."

Flushed with adrenaline, all I could repeat was "Oh my god, oh my god" (the irony was not lost on me) until he asked me where I was headed.

I replied, "St John's," as my head shouted, *Think of something smart to say!* I so wanted to tell him that Alan Grafen, his doctoral student, thought highly of me, but I resisted the urge to name-drop. Instead, I asked if he— Richard Dawkins—would take a selfie with me.

"A selfie?" He raised an eyebrow.

He didn't say no, so I fumbled for my digital camera and took a photo with the flash on. When we drove up to my college, I asked if he wanted to come around for a drink. He politely declined. I thanked him for the ride and went to my room, buzzing.

Hannah, who had been left behind at the train station, joined me not long after in her own cab. This was my unexpected "outing." But Hannah was not bitter. She said she'd always known. I showed her my photo with Richard Dawkins. He and I are pressing our heads together. I have a big smile. It almost looks like he is smiling too.

23

The last thing I remembered was having drinks in my room with a Korean girl in the year below me. My closest friends were from my college, but I was friendly with the Korean community and attended the main events organized each term by the Korean Society. This was K-pop night, and we were going to head out to a nightclub.

Looking around now, I found myself lying on a hospital bed in a silent, darkened room. The last time I had woken like this, after smoking weed in Paris, my parents had been there. This time, two men in black were sitting against a wall, waiting for me to regain consciousness. After exchanging a few words, they escorted me down into a police car. I figured they would drop me back at college. Instead, we arrived at the police station, where I was ordered to take off my jacket and hand in my belongings. Without explanation, I was thrown inside a cell and locked behind a heavy door that shut with a loud clank. It was foul in there. In one corner was a revolting metal toilet without a seat. In another was a solid piece of metal—the bed. Nowhere else to go, I lay on top and drifted off, wondering what I could have possibly done to end up in there.

When I came to, I had no idea how long I'd been asleep or if anyone was coming to get me. I knocked on the metal door, but no response came. I tried banging it this time, but still nothing. The lack of response terrified me. All I could hear was some noise from the adjacent cells. To get someone's attention, I started pounding the door with both hands and screaming, "I'm thirsty! Please bring me some water!" Finally, a guard slipped a small plastic cup through the sliding window on the metal door. I downed it and asked for more, but that was it.

After what must have been a few hours, though I had no way of telling, someone came to take me to another room. I was glad to finally leave the cell, even if it was to have my mugshot and fingerprints taken. Next step was a DNA test. "I am *not* doing that," I said emphatically. But they weren't asking for my permission. After forcibly accepting the swab, as if I were some murder suspect, I was taken to a minuscule interrogation room. A female officer came in and asked me what I remembered from the previous night. When I told her I couldn't remember anything, she told me that I had in fact "punched" a police officer.

"What? That can't be true," I said. I have never been a violent person, drunk or sober, and found that difficult to believe. To prove herself, she played some CCTV footage. I recognized myself in it. I am sitting outside the nightclub with some friends whom I can't make out, and a police officer comes over, apparently asking if there's any trouble. I try to stand, but I'm so drunk I need to be propped up. My limbs are like tentacles. Then I lurch and flail my arm, which hits the tip of the officer's cap, and her cap falls off.

I was shocked to see the video and told the officer that I couldn't remember any of it—not that that was any excuse—and that I was sorry for my behavior. I also told her that what I had done could not be described as "punching." But that was not up for debate. She insisted that I had and laid out my options for me: I could either be "let off" with a caution or go to court and dispute this but risk ending up with a conviction. It was clear she was steering me towards the former. I didn't know what the difference between a caution and a conviction was, but the last thing I wanted was to go to court, so I accepted the caution. In fact, I was given two cautions: for being "drunk and disorderly" and "assaulting a constable."

A few days later, I delivered a handwritten card addressed to the constable, apologizing for my reprehensible behavior and ultimately asking if there was any way that the cautions could be removed from my records. A rather lengthy response came through my college letterbox from Sergeant 83021, who was apparently present on the evening of my arrest. He told me that I was "rude, abusive, aggressive and drunk"; my behavior was "atrocious"; my actions were "inconsiderate and indeed criminal." It would seem from his letter that I really "hurt" this constable by "punching her to the mouth."

My whole body tensed reading this. What I had done was wrong, shameful and irresponsible. I should never have gotten so drunk. But hand on heart, I did not punch anyone; I flailed my arm and her cap fell off. What did this sergeant achieve by branding me a criminal? I was a twenty-one-year-old university student who had gotten too drunk. The response seemed so vicious and disproportionate.

I learned the hard way that a caution is a permanent record retained indefinitely on the Police National Computer, something that would stain my background check with new employers and something I needed to clear with every application to the Home Office. Years later, when I wanted to become a student mentor at an underprivileged school, the cautions came up on my background check and I needed a special dispensation confirming that I was of sound character and no threat to the students.

That night, I lost my passport—my last diplomatic passport—which I'd brought as ID to enter the nightclub. I wondered if it would have conferred diplomatic immunity and if that might have had anything to do with its disappearance. Growing up, at airport immigration, we followed the special "diplomats" sign rather than queuing with everyone else. And when I was younger and had to travel by myself, my dad would be waiting for me right when I got off the plane because he could get through airport security even when he wasn't flying. I felt special in those moments. Now, my navy-blue diplomatic passport would be replaced with the standard dark green one. More than anything, it felt like I was no longer under the wing of my dad's protection, something I had taken for granted.

24

As much as I enjoyed my first two years and even the first term of my third and final year at Oxford, there would be no degree without finals: seven grueling three-hour exams. Which meant I was no longer studying for the pure joys of learning but as a means to an end, to get a good mark. It seemed all that mattered in these last few months was how I did in finals.

During my last term, I tacked a piece of paper with "2:1" written in large letters in my room. I didn't need a First, I told myself. I "just" needed a two-one, which is considered a respectable grade and often required by reputable employers. But as much as I tried to manage my own expectations, the pressure felt intense. I didn't know where it was coming from. My parents would be happy as long as I graduated. Nor was I worrying about jobs at this point. It must have come from within, this fear of failure, something ingrained in me from a young age, going back to the terror I felt as a ten-year-old during my math grade incident in Malaysia.

Seeing how depressed I was during my last trip to Norway, when I'd had my emergency consultation, my mom wrote to me:

Please don't stress over exams—this kind of thing will not sway your life. If anything, it'll have a minuscule impact on your happiness. If it's ever too much, just let it down. Take a rest or just let it go entirely.

But I couldn't rest or let it go. In the months leading up to finals, I was necking almost two bottles of red wine each evening. I called my mom for help, and she flew over straight away to stay with me for a couple of days. Even with her by my side, I continued to drink heavily. There was nothing she could do to moderate my consumption.

One night after my mom went to bed, I rambled to the shared kitchen—invariably drunk by this time—and found a big loaf of artisan bread by the windowsill. I tore off a piece, stuck it in the toaster and dozed off. Moments later, I was woken by the smell of something burning. When I looked up, there was a small flame in the toaster, the size of one on a Bunsen burner. I rushed to turn the tap on and threw as much water as I could. The flame was extinguished, but the smoke was everywhere and triggered the fire alarm. "Was it you?" my mom asked when I scurried back to my room. She didn't need me to respond. We sat in silence, except for the sound of footsteps evacuating. Then came a knock at the door. It was the porters. I denied having anything to do with it, trying to look frustrated by the pandemonium in the middle of the night, but everyone knew, including those who had to sit their finals the very next day.

My mom left a note for me on the back of a bus timetable before she returned to Norway. She told me how hard it was leaving me here knowing what a difficult time I was having and, worse, knowing there was nothing she could do to make me feel better. She wrote:

> *You might be busy getting on with your life, then suddenly wonder, who am I, what am I doing, for whom and to what end am I living like this? Is there any meaning to this? Even if I were to fail, or if I were to die, or even if something bigger were to happen, it's only for an instant, it has no impact on the universe, the Earth will keep rotating as they say... Even someone as dull as me has these kinds of thoughts every now and again, so I can only imagine what it's like for a sensitive child like you.*

I was reduced to tears. I'd never verbalized my meaning-of-life issues to my mom—or anyone—in this way, but she understood exactly how I felt. She went on:

> *My beautiful baby Lena,*
>
> *There was recently an earthquake in China. I read that under all the rubble, mothers were protecting their children in their arms. Some were fortunate to live; others died. If anything like that were to ever happen to me, I would hold you tight a hundred times, a thousand times over to make sure you lived. Whatever I can do to save you, I will do it.*
>
> *Please don't forget that whatever you are thinking and feeling now can change unrecognizably with time. I know this will sound trite and I'm sorry that this is all I can say, that I am not more capable, but time will heal...*

Please have faith. No, keep telling this to yourself. There will absolutely be a day when you are smiling again. I miss you already.

Umma

~

I counted down the days, wishing I could speed up time. A few months earlier, one of my tutors had suggested I consider rusticating, or dropping to the year below. He thought it would be a shame to do poorly in my finals due to stress, given how well I'd done until then. But I couldn't bear the thought of prolonging this pressure and anxiety for another year. I just wanted to get it over with.

Finally, it was time. Dressed in my gown and sub fusc— white shirt, black skirt, black ribbon around my collar—I headed to the Examination Schools. In keeping with tradition, I wore a white carnation for my first exam. Hundreds of us piled into the cavernous room laid out with rows and rows of desks, everyone full of nervous energy. I sat upright in my assigned seat, right in the middle of the room, with only my pen and mortarboard, trying to drown out the sound of the shuffling feet, shaking legs and tapping pens all around me.

The second the invigilator wished us luck, I dived into the exam like a swimmer responding to the sound of a starting pistol going off. Even though I had a tendency to crumble under longer-term pressure, like the weeks and months leading up to exams, I could excel under acute pressure. It felt like new synapses were forming in my brain as my hands flew furiously across the blank pages. I knew I only had one hour per question, so tried to be selective about what I wanted to say. I also kept reminding myself of one piece of advice I'd received: "Don't write like a girl." It was misogynistic, but the point was taken. Be assertive.

Now just six more to go...

I felt like a marathon runner who'd just broken through the final tape to the cheering crowds when I came out of the Examination Schools for the last time, red carnation pinned to my gown. My friends were waiting for me for the final Oxford experience: trashing. They sprayed me with whipping cream and threw all kinds of liquids on me, which I later washed off by jumping into a pond in University Parks. It felt most liberating.

The exams seemed to have gone well overall, though you could never really tell. To be honest, I didn't care. I was so relieved to have just finished. No. More. Exams. Ever.

~

A month later, I was on a road trip in Belgium with my mom and some family friends when my phone pinged with a notification that our results had been released. "They're out," I exclaimed. Although I told myself I didn't care what mark I got, I'd been checking my phone anxiously the last couple of days. My mom pulled off the highway and stopped at the first gas station so I could check my results. While she pretended to refill the car, I walked away for some privacy. Hands trembling, I entered my log-in details and waited for the results to load.

"Holy shit" was all I could say. A clear first-class degree. I couldn't believe my eyes. Beaming, I skipped back to my mom. She could see I had good news. The mood in the car was one of euphoria when we got back on the highway.

Then, less than half an hour later, I received an email from the course administrator saying that I had come top of my class. As a bonus, I also won an award for the best dissertation. Was I dreaming? I stuck my head out the backseat window and whooped and whooped and whooped. My mom, who was driving, was in tears of joy.

25

As my time at Oxford came to an end, so did my dad's posting to Norway. After five years abroad, including two years in Paris, he was repatriated, which meant I, too, returned to Korea, my "home" by default.

It felt like the ultimate triumphant return. When I had left Korea, I was the troublemaker, the errant child. Here I was, not only an Oxford graduate, but I'd come top of my class. I felt vindicated. I'm not sure to whom I wanted to prove myself so much, but I hoped my mom could at least hold her head high in front of friends and family. I was not a lost cause.

Each move demanded a host of adjustments, but our lives changed even more drastically this time. I had always known the ambassadorial lifestyle—having a chef, a cleaner and a driver—would be fleeting. I knew the crockery, the furniture, the treadmill, the vases, the paintings at the residence, none of it was ours. An officer had come to do the inventory before our departure. We'd also always made a point of keeping our private lives separate. My dad drove his silver Audi instead of the official car on weekends; my mom kept separate stashes of receipts to distinguish our day-to-day expenditure from entertainment expenses. Still, it was a big adjustment reverting to a normal life, our old life.

We moved into a cozy three-bedroom apartment in northeast Seoul, where most of my mom's side of the family lived. Instead of having wrought iron gates protecting our residence, we now had to worm through a busy supermarket to take the elevator up as the deal of the day was shouted on loudspeakers: "We've got huge watermelons for just 20,000 won today, that's right, ma'am, just 20,000 won for these sweet, juicy watermelons." Our new apartment felt claustrophobic compared to the double-height ceiling we'd become accustomed to in Oslo. Our balcony was stacked high with cardboard boxes, stuff there just wasn't space for after downsizing.

No longer the ambassador, my dad became the president of some organization under the Ministry of Education, though family friends still addressed him as "Mr. Ambassador" out of respect. My mom no longer regularly hosted luncheons and dinner parties, and now had to cook for my dad, though I think a part of her enjoyed taking back control of the kitchen. She seemed happy to return to Korea, running from engagement to engagement, busy reconnecting with all her old friends.

My brother had just completed his mandatory military service—twenty-four months in the air force—after graduating from college. While I imagined him in the cockpit, the closest he got to an aircraft in reality was to shovel snow off the runway so the jets could take off. Even though we were all in Korea now, my brother didn't live with us. After he was discharged, he became a pro gamer. No one, least of all my parents, could have imagined he would make a career out of video games, but they were surprisingly open-minded, even my dad. *Dota 2* being a "team sport" with five players—it was difficult for us to get used to the idea of esports—my brother trained with his teammates in Incheon.

As for me, I had no plans. I had given little thought to life after finals, but I wasn't too worried. Everyone seemed to say, "The world's your oyster!"

～

The question was always, "What do you want to be when you grow up?" On the flight to Malaysia, I had decided I wanted to become a "stew-uh-dess." A little older, after changing my mind many times, I scribbled "bio-act" when we had to write down our dream jobs at a career session in high school. Although it sounds like some probiotic, it was my secret code for biologist or actress. I was always private about my goals because I felt revealing them would doom me to public failure, besides being embarrassed about having them in the first place. The problem was, "when you grow up" was no longer a hypothetical time in the distant future—I was supposedly a grown-up now—and neither a biologist nor an actress seemed like a realistic prospect. What did I want to be?

I had no clue. As much as I loved my degree, it had no immediate practical application. What employer would care for my thoughts on the nature versus nurture debate? And after going through finals, I had no desire, nor means, to do

174

further studies. The "Oxford bubble" had burst.

Throughout my upbringing, my mom always emphasized how I could do *anything* I wanted, how much potential I had. I brushed it off every time. She was my mom; she was obviously going to say that. My dad had no such belief in me but occasionally offered his ideas: "How about a schoolteacher or a professor? That's not so bad for a woman." Neither parent was helpful.

Within weeks of returning to Korea, I was filled with anxiety. As I mindlessly flicked through my phone one day, I saw a Facebook post by a university friend who was looking for someone to replace him as an intern at a major Korean broadcaster. I instantly put my hand up as I needed work experience on my résumé and something to tide me over until I secured a permanent role. Plus, it was a paid internship—a rarity—and would be enough to cover pocket money.

The program I worked on was a business news channel. Every morning a few clips from the American CNBC would be aired, and my job was to write Korean subtitles to these. The program aired live at 6 a.m., which meant I had to report by 4 a.m. The office was empty at that hour except for the two news anchors and production staff. I knew nothing about business or finance, so I struggled to understand the clips even in English. What was Jim Cramer ranting about on *Mad Money*? What was the Federal Reserve called in Korean? I didn't even know what the Fed was. Every morning, I ran against the clock to prepare the subtitles, ensuring my translation fit neatly into two rows for the screen.

I headed home when most people were commuting in, then applied for jobs, indiscriminately: everything from investment banks and insurance companies to publishing houses, boutique M&A outfits, hotels, retail stores and pharmaceuticals. It seemed the best strategy when I didn't know what I wanted to do. Most applications were to the UK, but I also applied to the US and other English-speaking countries, wherever I could find vacancies. It seemed a full-time job doing the research, drafting cover letters—desperately pitching my deep interpersonal and problem-solving skills—and reconfiguring my résumé to fill as much space with my limited experience.

In the afternoon, my boyfriend would check up on me, asking how many applications I had submitted that day. Paul had courted me for months at Oxford, but I hadn't been interested. Paul was petite and had a hairline that had already receded past the crown of his head, not that either of those factors particularly bothered me. It was his over-the-top poshness I didn't take to. He was what I considered a stereotypically British public schoolboy. He wore perfectly tailored suits from Savile Row, with a silk pocket square from Hermès or, if in casual wear, a perfectly pressed shirt with cufflinks and a Barbour jacket on top. He literally wore red trousers. Besides his immaculate dress code, Paul came across as too "proper"—his grammar was perfect, full stops at the end of each sentence, even when texting. I found that annoying. But he was persistent—in the most gentlemanly way—until my very last day at Oxford when we had a few too many drinks in fancy oversized wine glasses at his place and ended up kissing. That developed over the summer, and I was now in a long-distance relationship with him. I guess I have a knack for falling in love at the last minute. Although

I had dated since Yoonhak, I don't think I was in love again until Paul.

Paul had read Law at Christ Church, the "Harry Potter" college with a reputation for being posh, but he had no interest in becoming a lawyer. Like me, he wasn't sure what to do with the rest of his life, though deep down I think he always knew he wanted to become a police officer. I couldn't see the attraction, especially after my "incident" at Oxford, but he'd always had a fundamental respect for authority, law and order, and wanted to serve the community. But for now, he was in the trenches with me. "I always fail because my heart's not in it," he wrote to me after receiving yet another rejection from a management consultancy role he didn't even want.

Looking back, I feel this period "fresh" out of university is mis-sold. People love to say: *What an exciting time when you're young, bright and beautiful. You should live your life, achieve your dreams, follow your passion.* As if that was easy. The reality for me was, the more applications I submitted, the more rejections I received; most companies never even replied. Sometimes rejections appeared from companies I had forgotten I even applied to, but it was no less demoralizing. Was I so unemployable? How much experience was a recent graduate meant to have? Wasn't my academic record enough to show that I was hardworking? I suppose I had a sense of entitlement: I deserved a good job after all that hard work. At school, we were told to study hard to get into a good university, as if that guaranteed a successful future. But life did not seem to sort itself out like I felt I'd been promised. I felt let down, deceived.

It was only then that I realized the importance of visas. Growing up, I had a diplomatic passport and followed my parents around the world without once worrying about the need for a visa. It was news to me that most countries had stringent entry requirements for long-term stays. I didn't know that most of the companies I had applied to in the UK didn't even have the authority to sponsor visas. Not only had I wasted my time and energy, but the existence of borders suddenly felt like a gross injustice. Of course, I recognize my immense privilege here: there are circumstances far more dire and desperate than mine, not least migrants and refugees who are literally fighting for their survival.

As it was looking less likely that I would get a job outside Korea, I started considering roles within Korea as a last resort. I soon learned that Korean résumés required details of your parents' ages and occupations, your sibling relationship, whether you and your siblings had completed your military service. They even required a headshot. I couldn't imagine myself working in a country that asked for such details. Paul also looked into getting a job in Korea but they all seemed to require teaching experience or knowledge of Korean, neither of which he had.

As the rejections piled in, my sense of urgency heightened. I didn't like the feeling of being beholden to my dad as the provider and was desperate for financial independence. When I was at university, my dad would refer to me as the "money-munching hippo" in reference to my Oxford tuition fees. He may have intended it as a humble brag, an endearing way to boast to guests his daughter was studying at Oxford, but it made me feel like a huge financial burden. I was not some rich international student; my parents were spending all their savings on my higher education. This guilt made me feel resentful.

My mom watched me agonize over the problem of what to do with the rest of my life, tiptoeing around me as I constantly lashed out. It didn't help that my circadian rhythm was out of whack. I was eating at random hours and drinking *maehwasu*, a Korean plum wine, from the early afternoon. That was my "evening" as I had to wake up at 3 a.m. for the internship. My mom believed the night shifts were not worth it—I was jeopardizing my mental and physical health. With the perspective of an adult, she wished I would take it easy and tried to talk me out of the internship.

"You just don't get it, do you? How am I going to get a job with nothing on my résumé?" I flipped out at my mom. I hate to say it, but I thought, *What would you know, you're a housewife, you clearly don't understand the job market.*

Of the countless roles I applied for, only a few progressed to the telephone interview stage, so I was elated when I managed to secure one with a Big Four accounting firm. I prepared for hours, scouring the internet for tips, practicing picking up the phone in a professional tone: "Hi, Lena Lee speaking." I kicked my parents out of the apartment for the interview. When the recruiter asked at the end if there was anything else I wanted to add, I teared up as I reiterated my interest in—no, my passion for—the role. My desperation must have come across as I was invited to interview in person at their offices.

I was flown to London and happy to see Paul. Although our relationship had been mostly long-distance at this point,

Paul cared for me so consistently throughout those first months together. Over Skype, he would ask me what I was up to, how I was doing and listen to all my frustrations about my family, the internship and the latest rejection. He would tell me how much he loved me and that he missed me terribly. He sent me emails telling me that I was the most wonderful person, saying how lucky he was to have me, and that he hoped we would spend decades happily together until we died. I don't know how I would have survived without Paul's emotional support. It was nice to be physically together now. I'd missed his body, his hairy chest, his perfectly round butt and surprisingly muscular build under his petite frame.

But focus! I was there for the final stages of the interview process. Dressed in a black trouser suit, I arrived early—but not too early—and waited in the reception area, watching staff touch in and out of the entrance gates. When my interviewer, a well-groomed white man, came to collect me, I had my right hand ready to shake his hand, with a grip that conveyed confidence. I knew the interview went well. We talked about my global upbringing. When I had to talk business, I spoke about Samsung, which I knew I had an edge on purely by virtue of being Korean. After we'd chatted for an hour, he said, rolling his eyes, "Gosh, I'm supposed to ask you, what are your strengths and weaknesses?" My weakness was obviously that I was a perfectionist. I wanted to open a bottle of champagne that day, but Paul said we should wait.

A few days later, while still in London, I received a call offering me a role on the graduate program starting the next September. I tried not to squeal until I hung up. I had finally secured my first real job. More importantly, I had my ticket to London.

I felt giddy about starting a new chapter of my life. After a promising start, I had had the most miserable year in Korea and was ready to leave, move on. I vowed not to return for at least the next three years, though I didn't say this to my grandma when she asked, "When will I see you again?"

PART FOUR

New Roots

2014 to the present day

26

LONDON, ENGLAND, 2014 (age 23)

Paul greeted me with open arms and a wide grin as I pushed my cart through the sliding doors at Heathrow. I had made it. No, *we* had made it. Paul was accepted to the fast-track scheme in the Metropolitan Police but decided to "play it safe" by joining the Big Four. He coincidentally secured a job at the same firm as me, though in a different part of the business. It was, after all, one of the largest graduate employers.

We strode hand in hand to our first day of work, a welcome event held in a vast ballroom at a five-star hotel. Excitement filled the air as we contemplated our new lives together as proper adults with proper jobs. Paul wore a suit and tie—his usual attire—but I felt like I was playing dress-up in my pencil skirt and black heels. Hundreds of us graduates looked up at the stage with hopeful eyes, invigorated by the cheesy music and lighting effects. We heard a lot about adding value, building trust in society and doing the right thing. Some partners came to tell us about their path to partnership, and I felt genuinely inspired to embark on my own journey as a career woman.

I moved into a modern studio in Borough, a trendy area

only a ten-minute walk from the office I had interviewed at. Paul had kindly attended the viewing and sorted out the admin on my behalf. The rent was much too expensive for the graduate pay I would be on—I'd need to use my savings—but I reasoned this was a big move and wanted to minimize the controllable stressors like a long commute and any potential flatmate trouble. What I hadn't realized was that my job would require me to commute not to the office but to client sites, the first of which was in Staines: two Tube journeys, a train and a company shuttle bus ride away. It took an hour and half each way. I couldn't fathom how my dad had coped driving to and from Manhattan every day.

We were at the client site to do "face time," but my work as an audit junior consisted primarily of ticking and tying numbers. I would ask the client for a sample of invoices and ensure the details (e.g., invoice number 90283741) matched the records on a spreadsheet. Fun times, not to mention great use of my higher education. Then, my "in-charge," someone two or three years more senior, would review my work and set me up for my next task. How I hated that term: in-charge. It was a young team, everyone in their early to mid-twenties, but I really didn't enjoy the atmosphere. It felt claustrophobic, a dozen of us squished into a crowded room. I didn't get their "banter" and just wished for the day to end. "Was there anything else you needed me to do today?" I'd ask my in-charge at 5:30 p.m. as I shut my laptop, my passive-aggressive way of saying, "Sorry but not sorry, I'm off."

Back at the welcome event, everyone had been ultra-sociable, asking one another which "uni" they had gone to, keen to make a good first impression. It felt like freshers' week all over again. Within the first week, though, groups were formed along ethnic lines, like oil and water forming two separate layers. There was a dominant white group with a few posh brown boys, a mostly Muslim group, and an East Asian group. I think the metaphor is apt: it's not that the water doesn't like the oil and vice versa, but that the water molecules are attracted to each other. I was still astonished to see such a clear racial divide in the workplace. I was the only Korean person and became close friends with Sabi, a Nepali girl who I was instantly drawn to. Otherwise, I struggled to fit in.

As part of my three-year graduate contract, I had to qualify as a chartered accountant, which involved passing fifteen exams over three years—not what I had in mind when I finished my finals, but I figured it couldn't be nearly as stressful. It might even be interesting to learn about something different.

Not so, I wholly underestimated the amount of work required. The syllabus was huge and challenging for someone like me with no background in business or finance. Still, I preferred exams to being an auditor—anything seemed better—and I enjoyed getting time off as study leave. The pressure was real, though, as we could get fired if we failed the same exam twice. The day I finished my final exam, a four-hour, open-book case study, I decided to cut my hair short to signal yet another new start. I showed the hairdresser a picture of Scarlett Johansson in a pixie cut and ended up looking like a Korean boy.

By this time, I had moved permanently to a different role within the firm, which was office-based, already a huge improvement. For a change, I liked my team. There were no cliques. My colleagues were good at their jobs and fun to work with. I enjoyed the team socials, from Zorbing and Go Karting to going to comedy clubs and playing crazy golf. And the drinks afterwards. The guys tended to have beer—I could never understand how Brits drink outside pubs even in the middle of winter, holding their pints with frosty, purple fingers—and the ladies mostly wine. When I could get away with it, I ordered prosecco. I enjoyed drinking with my colleagues—I was always the one going, "C'mon, don't be boring. Have another drink!"—though was careful not to get drunk-drunk. One upside to being an experienced drinker, having started at the age of thirteen, was that I'd already done plenty of stupid things when drunk-drunk. I knew my limits, though that didn't mean I drank less than anyone else. Colleagues commented on my strong tolerance for someone so "small" (and Asian).

Objectively, I had a decent job with decent pay. I wasn't burned out by long hours nor suffering a toxic boss like some of my friends, especially in law, were. I just struggled with the meaninglessness of it all. My job was to value private businesses, which involved forecasting future cash flows, discounting those to a present value and cross-checking that against the public stock markets. The valuation methodology is underpinned by a whole lot of financial theory and widely adopted by investment bankers and finance professionals alike, across industries and around the world. To me, the whole thing seemed like a house of cards. It felt preposterous—however reasonable, supportable and defensible each and every assumption was—trying to forecast the level of profit a company would generate in, say, 2038. I would zone out when my colleagues debated technical details full of jargon, and was never sure if they truly cared about these things or if they'd somehow managed to convince themselves that they did, in order to get on in life—with life.

Looking back, I should never have been searching for that elusive "meaning" from this job, but I was, and felt despairing. What was the endgame? My next bonus and promotion? I wasn't even saving up. Even after the long-awaited salary boost post-qualification, most of my earnings were being spent on rent (and alcohol). In my darkest days, it occurred to me: I would rather sell my body than my soul. Life seemed like a never-ending ladder, a treadmill, a hamster wheel. It was like waiting for Godot.

I'd been right all along. The thing is, even as I submitted application after application, and as much as I had desperately wanted a job back in Korea, I knew I had no interest in a soulless corporate job. It would merely be my ticket out of Korea.

Maybe school days were the best days of my life after all.

~

I have never had anything like a childhood home, a door frame marked with my height over the years. Instead, I lived in all kinds of homes, from the big clapboard house in New Jersey to the Haussmann apartment in Paris, all temporary dwellings we rented when we were abroad. As tenants, we never even got to choose the paint color in our rooms. Back in America, my bedroom walls were spanned by a children's animal print, with giraffes, elephants and zebras. The most I could do as a young teen was tape over it with full-page ads ripped from women's magazines.

Even when we were back in Korea, we were "homeless," as my parents liked to say. Due to some financial mismanagement and poor luck, we always rented. Korea has a unique rental system whereby, instead of paying monthly rent, tenants put down an enormous deposit worth up to 90 percent of the market value of the house. The deposit is returned at the end of the lease term, which is typically two years, which meant we had to move house even within a three-year stint. As a result, three years was the longest we ever stayed at one address. I couldn't have imagined when I moved to London that staying three years in one place would be a dream.

Soon after starting my new job, it became obvious that there was no point living by myself in a modern apartment in Zone 1 when I spent most of my time commuting. My colleagues assumed I was some rich Asian kid whose parents were bankrolling me. In reality, my savings were dwindling fast, and I couldn't afford to stay there. My good-natured landlord let me cut my six-month contract short and thus began my long journey with SpareRoom, a website to find flatshares in London.

I found a cheap room next to a railway line in Southwark, not far from where I'd been living. It was on the ground floor of a decrepit block of flats with dark brown bricks, once-white windowpanes and black pipes running outside. "CITY OF LONDON HOUSING" was emblazoned on the side, just below the official coat of arms. I knocked on the numberless green door, unsure what to expect. At the time,

I didn't even know what a council estate was. A middle-aged lady with leathery skin and heavy-lidded eyes greeted me affably and invited me in. I was immediately overwhelmed by the stench of mothballs and cigarettes. Introducing herself as Mila, she asked me how old I was and what I did for a living. She seemed delighted to tell me that her son—I'd seen on the advert she had a son—was the same age as me, as if she wanted to set me up with him. I'd assumed he was a schoolboy. I didn't probe into their circumstances, but Mila would be letting out her room and sleeping on the wall bed in the living room where we were speaking. Her son had his own room. After briefly vetting each other, she showed me to "my" room, which was painted forest green and lit by a bare bulb. There was a Bob Marley poster over the bed and random trinkets and vases along a ledge. It was not ideal—I hadn't even met her son yet—but it cost less than half of what I had been paying, inclusive of bills. Mila asked me to pay a week's rent in cash as deposit and pay my rent, also in cash, every week. I accepted.

Mila was Croatian and had moved to London when her son was little. She was a cleaner and nanny for various households and seemed genuinely fond of the children she looked after. When she cooked, she always offered me some Croatian bean stew and burek filo pastries. Her son smoked weed and played computer games all day, while priding himself on being an intellectual. He often called his mother by her last name. Their relationship reminded me of that between Ignatius and his mother in *A Confederacy of Dunces*.

During this time, my dad was posted as the Korean ambassador to UNESCO, which is headquartered in Paris.

The assignment was orchestrated to be near me, and I often used the Eurostar to visit my parents. Their new residence was a high-ceilinged apartment in the exclusive suburb of Neuilly-sur-Seine, the Bois de Boulogne on their doorstep. As in Norway, they had a chef, a cleaner—Ajumma had followed them back to Paris—and a driver. When Mila asked me what my father did, I kept it vague: "He's a civil servant, you know, works for the government."

Once, my parents drove up from Paris to visit me. Seeing only the exterior of the council estate, my dad walked away, shaking his head. I could almost hear him tsking. My mom came inside, but I could tell she was trying her best to conceal her pity as she witnessed my living conditions. I felt so small. I knew my parents weren't judging me; they just felt sorry for me. My mom would repeatedly apologize to me that she couldn't support me better financially even though I didn't want or expect anything from them. I wanted to be independent.

Every now and again, Mila liked to treat herself to new home accessories. When she hung a butterfly wind chime on the front door—next to the existing "Home Sweet Home" sign—I asked if she could put it elsewhere as it was affecting my sleep. I thought I was being honest and direct with her, as she had asked me to be, but for some reason she was greatly offended. It was a minor dispute, but I ended up moving out on short notice after a year and a half of cordial relations.

Back on SpareRoom, I found a three-bedroom flat in Canary Wharf, the finance district, and arranged a viewing with the estate agent. The room looked as advertised: plain, impersonal and cheaply furnished. The living area had been converted into a third bedroom, and the shared kitchen had no window or natural light. But I knew my budget would only stretch so far and was excited the place came with a basement gym and indoor pool, albeit a small one. I swiftly paid the deposit and signed the contract, not having met either of my flatmates. The agent had reassured me that they were both nice young male professionals, and I took him at his word.

My mom came from Paris to help me move and seemed pleased with the apparent upgrade from the council flat. In some ways, it was an improvement. I no longer had the musky smell of Mila's place seeping into my clothes. I no longer had to shiver in the cold shower. I could use the washing machine without the kitchen sink gurgling up with dirty backwash and leaving behind slugs. But I was still boxed into my little room, which only had a small window that hinged at the top and barely pushed open a few inches. My windowsill served as my "TV" stand, where I perched my work laptop and streamed Netflix, the white neon lights of the J.P. Morgan building glowing in the background. Cars and motorcycles regularly vroomed outside with their obnoxious wheel spins. I accepted this as the reality of living in Central London.

The real problem started when not long after I moved in, the boy I shared a bathroom with moved out and a replacement came. He allegedly ran a one-man real estate shop. At first, he seemed perfectly nice. Soon enough, he was using all my kitchen ingredients and leaving a dirty pile of my own dishes in the sink. He pissed all over our shared toilet and clogged it with his shit and reams of toilet paper. I cleaned up after him. When I could no longer stand the smell of weed saturating our flat, I asked him to open his window. He didn't. I am pretty sure from his dodgy demeanor and the phone calls I overheard that he was a drug dealer. One night, he brought back a couple of girls who I could hear whispering loudly and cackling outside my room. They were shuffling in and out of the bathroom all night. Two of them were still there in the morning, looking bleary-eyed. One had frizzy hair and was wearing a crop top, her chubby belly on display. She looked so young, maybe sixteen at most. I confronted the other one, who looked older and scarily unsavory. She called me a "bitch" and accused me of lying. This was too much to put up with on a Monday morning. I was back on SpareRoom.

My mom came from Paris to help me move, again. I found these moves stressful and overwhelming, but for my mom, they were trifling compared to the international moves she was used to. It was just one room's worth of boxes and bags and some kitchenware, across London, in a van, compared to an entire household in containerships not to be seen for months. I realized how much I had been shielded from the enormous administrative burden of moving countries.

The next flatshare was back in Southwark with two Indian boys, one Indian-American and one Indian-British, who knew each other through their moms. I had qualified as a chartered accountant and received a pay rise by this time, so made sure to get an en suite. My room was much more spacious, and the boys were easy to live with. We respected one another's space and went for civil dinners together. But before my mom returned to Paris, she blurted out, "Why does the bathroom fan whir like that? The boys don't clean up, do they?"

"Can you stop complaining for once?" I exploded. "It's not perfect. I just make do, okay?"

When my contract expired, my mom came to help me move yet again. I found an ex-council flat, only a three-minute walk from the office. I lived with a lady named Simona, who was the same age as my mom but looked like Sharon Stone—tall and toned, with short blonde hair. Despite my initial reservations about living with the landlady, Simona was pleasant to live with. She was Romanian and had grown up under the communist Ceaușescu regime. She had gone to a kibbutz-style school, where she met her husband. They were happily married until he wanted children, and she started having nightmares about them. So they got divorced.

Simona was proud of her career and would tell me how she changed her job at least every three years and how she dealt with difficult male bosses. She said she'd been a workaholic and alcoholic and told me how happy she was with her life, perhaps in hindsight a little too often for it to be truly convincing. She liked to tell me that the reason she let out her spare room was not for cash but to help someone out. But when I gave her notice to move out as I had found a new job in a different area of London, she became unexpectedly short with me. Despite her emphasizing how happy she was, I think she may have been rather lonely.

In five years, I ended up living in five different flats. This was not the glamorous life of a career woman I had envisioned at the orientation. I compared myself to my peers. Some were in flatshares like me, though they seemed to be living with friends or siblings, not random people. Others like Paul were living at home. A few had "got on the property ladder" and bought their first homes with support from the Bank of Mum and Dad.

I regretted choosing London, one of the most expensive cities in the world, not that there was much choice.

~

I had friends—good friends—including Hannah and others from university, as well as some work friends like Sabi, whom I'd meet up with for dinner and catch up on life with. Sometimes it was nice to have someone to talk to, but often I couldn't be bothered. I hated the deafening screech of the Tube and it felt like too much effort just getting to and from the restaurant. I also had a habit of arriving at least ten to fifteen minutes early and would take it as a huge slight if anyone was just five minutes late. Little things like that vexed me disproportionately.

I was totally comfortable being by myself. At Oxford, I liked going to the cinema and attending talks and plays across the university by myself. I didn't even mind having lunch by myself in Hall to save me from engaging in small talk. I dreaded someone joining me, perhaps out of sympathy, especially towards the end of a meal, the whole thing of waiting for others to finish eating and all that. By this time, I was going on holiday by myself. It felt so much easier and simpler that way.

Paul was the closest person I had in London. In fact, if it wasn't for him, I probably would have given up on finding a job in the UK. Paul was—and is—a good person. He still told me several times a day how beautiful I was and how much he loved me. When we walked up the stairs, me always before him, he would tell me, almost unable to stop himself, "Your calves are so beautiful." I hated my big, fat calves. "Stop taking the piss," I'd say. But he truly meant it. He made me feel like I was loved unconditionally—not just my calves but everything about me, despite all my flaws.

I'm not sure what Paul saw in me because I was a mess, deep into my red wine phase, when he started courting me back at Oxford. Seeing my love of red wine, he invited me to tastings at the Wine Circle, a university society that feels the need to claim to be "not pretentious." I was concerned more with intoxication than appellations and vintages, but he treated me like I deserved better. He also went out of his way to build a good relationship with my parents. He had such a good understanding of my dad and would address him deferentially as "Your Excellency" and gift him fine wines, including a rare bottle of 1982 Château Cos d'Estournel. For my mom's birthday, Paul would deliver a beautiful box of fine chocolates, along with a handwritten card. My dad loved that Paul was old money; my mom, as much as she adored Paul, worried that my attraction to him might have something to do with the fact that he was the exact opposite of my dad (otherwise known as daddy issues).

The real problem was that Paul didn't have much time for me. Having chosen not to make policing his day job, he became a special constable, or a volunteer police officer. He would wear the same Met uniform and have the same powers as regular police officers, except he carried out his duties during his free time. Paul volunteered most weekends and bank holidays, working either all day and late into the evening or on night shifts, which he seemed to prefer as those often turned out to be more eventful. He loved patrolling Portobello Road Market, where thefts were common; his favorite was the Notting Hill Carnival. There was a minimum number of hours he had to complete annually as a special constable but Paul's level of commitment far exceeded that. His eyes would twinkle with childlike excitement when he recounted a previous night's arrest to me. I couldn't understand what he loved so much about it that he would prefer to spend his time policing than with me. To use the five love languages, I think Paul's way of giving love was with words of affirmation, which I couldn't fault him for, but what I needed more than anything was quality time together.

The way I dealt with this was by breaking up with him, then going on lots of Tinder dates. There was the German investment banker who took me to Nobu on our first date, then couldn't take no for an answer. The white British NHS doctor who spoke Korean remarkably well after a year abroad, but he played it up so much, I suspected he was preying on Korean girls. The Italian architect who I couldn't find anything in common with—I never understood the thing for Italian boys. The Korean-British guy who had gone to the same school as Paul and was building his own start-up. The civil servant who had an endearing Yorkshire accent but had never tried sushi before—that was a deal-breaker.

A Pakistani boy who seemed so confident on the app but couldn't make any conversation in person. It turned out he had never even kissed a girl and was lost without his friends drafting the messages for him.

I was hyper-attuned to race in the dating world. While I dated guys from different ethnicities, I was always trying to figure out if the non-Asians had yellow fever and if that was the only reason they had swiped right. I don't think there is anything wrong if a guy fancies Asian women. I went through a Middle Eastern phase where I dated guys from Lebanon, Iran and Palestine. The problem is racial hierarchy. A man once tried to compliment me at a coffee shop in Paris by saying, *"T'es belle, pour une asiatique"* (You're beautiful, for an Asian). That was unacceptable.

I had fun on many of these dates, but it was draining having to repeat the same old spiel about where I was from. I would go on a second and occasionally a third date but didn't connect meaningfully with anyone. Tinder was merely how I exerted control, to tell Paul, "I don't need you." But the truth was, the more dates I went on, the more I felt lost and the more I fell back on Paul. I did need him. I would call him after a date—it wasn't "cheating" because I'd technically broken up with him—and he would pick up every time. Whenever I broke up with him, Paul knew I was crying wolf and we would get back together in a few days, or at most, a few weeks.

I didn't have family in London: no siblings, parents, grandparents, cousins, aunts or uncles. I rejected friendships and tried to find solace in Tinder dates. I saw a therapist once, but I couldn't be bothered to fill her in on my life—

more than anything, I could tell she was intrigued by all the moving around and wanted to know more for her own curiosity's sake.

Whether I had brought this on myself, I was alone and deeply lonely.

27

My solution to all this—the meaninglessness of my corporate job, my unstable living situation, my loneliness—was none other than alcohol.

When I was seven or so, my grandpa offered me a sip of soju at a family gathering. My mom protested, but he batted her away. "It's alright, it's alright." I took a tiny cautious sip of the clear liquid and declared, "I am never drinking alcohol again."

As if. Now, as soon as I got home from work, I flicked my shoes off and hurried to the fridge, where a chilled bottle of bubbly greeted me like a dog wagging its tail, happy to see its owner come home. After unwrapping the foil, fumbling in my excitement, I would twist the cork until—*Pop!*—then inhale the "smoke" curling out.

Ahhhhh. The first sip felt like such a release, like when you first get into a warm bath or unzip a pair of tight trousers. I could finally breathe again. The alcohol coursed through my brain, allowing the neurons to reconfigure and snap into place. *Click.* Then it pumped through my body, radiating into each limb. I could be me now, no inhibitions or social niceties, no norms or expectations.

I *needed* this drink—not "wanted"; needed. I also deserved it. It was compensation for getting through the day, for holding it together. How could I spend all day doing mindbogglingly tedious work and *not* reward myself with a drink? I couldn't understand how everyone else did it. I remember coming home from work one day, having promised myself I would abstain that evening, but then when my phone flashed with an email requesting that I get something done immediately, I felt relieved. I now had a valid reason to drink.

It was never one drink. What would be the point of that? I knew I'd polish off at least one bottle. Whether to open the second bottle was the test—a test of my willpower and self-control—which I failed on most days. I felt a huge amount of guilt and self-loathing succumbing, but hey, since it was open…

By any measure, I'd be drunk. But by my own standards, "drunk" was when you were passed out on the street or just out of control. Aside from the time I was arrested, I rarely did things like that. My evenings were harmless, mostly spent watching Netflix in my room. There are so many films and TV shows I watched in a state of intoxicated stupor— *Gilmore Girls*, *Jane the Virgin*, *How I Met Your Mother*—I don't remember what happens in any of them. But the evenings just seemed so long without alcohol. I didn't know what to do with myself.

Sometimes I texted Paul when I was drinking. My messages would start off benign ("What are you up to?"), then turn cutesy as I hit my sweet spot ("How's Paulicing?"), then eventually turn into pure vitriol as I got more drunk and didn't receive any reply ("You're the worst thing that's ever happened to me. I wish I'd never met you. I hope you spend the rest of your life policing and die a lonely death."). Paul always remained calm and never stooped to my level.

Inevitably, I would wake up the next morning to the mess I'd created and be filled with regret and shame. I would tidy my room, open the windows and take out the empty bottles to destroy all physical evidence from the previous night's rampage. But I couldn't get rid of the hangover: head slightly pounding, the slight feeling of retching, the rocking back and forth, the numbness and nausea a normal part of my state of being.

I still showed up to work the next day, always on time. I was no star performer but I was responsible and got the job done. No one had to know that my night and day were like Jekyll and Hyde, as long as I was careful when stocking up. Except for the few dreadful months in Canary Wharf, I lived within walking distance from the office, so I fretted that a colleague might spot me checking out bottles at the local Tesco, though I could always make out that I was hosting a dinner party. I was so discreet that I'm not sure if even my flatmates knew about my nightly drinking; or maybe they did. My close friends knew I had a problem, Paul knew, and my parents knew, though no one knew the true extent of it. I would have balked if anyone had tried to suggest I needed help.

My social plans revolved around drinking. I didn't do coffee and had anxiety about the availability of alcohol at social gatherings. I always arrived early to engagements and would order drinks—often prosecco—for myself while I waited. I would have already checked the restaurant's drinks menu online, even if not the food menu. Annoyingly, a standard prosecco glass is only 125ml, 30 percent smaller than a standard wine glass, so even if I drank at the same pace as others (which I didn't), I would run out faster. I seldom waited for others to finish their drinks and instead of waiting for a lull in the conversation, I'd happily cut someone off mid-sentence to make sure I got the server's attention in time. Priorities.

I have always been good with money, but alcohol was compartmentalized differently in my brain. I might scrimp on a coffee but wouldn't think twice before ordering a £38 bottle at a restaurant. When others were doing rounds at a pub, I'd just buy an entire bottle. Alcohol was a non-negotiable expense. This was another reason I preferred drinking at home: it was so much cheaper.

When I drank socially, I had to stay alert and control my drinking, which I hated. Back at Oxford, this guy from Luxembourg who was an accomplished chef and wine connoisseur with a successful fine dining blog invited me to dinner in his college room one Valentine's Day. He cooked a fancy three-course meal for me, with lobster as the main, and opened some bottles he had stored under his bed. I could tell they were expensive, which meant I was supposed to sip— not gulp—them. After sharing two bottles—one white, one red—I was itching for more. He, of course, was hoping the night would take a romantic turn. Quarter to midnight, I bolted. I made it to Tesco in time to buy some cheap red wine and drank away in my room.

I had a habit of running to the shops like this just before they closed even when I was drinking by myself. Because the worst thing was to run out.

Alcohol wasn't my only addiction. I was also binge-eating. I think it started in earnest at Oxford when I would raid the communal fridges for ice cream, leftover pasta, whatever I could find in other people's Tupperware. I would gobble up uncooked vegetables and once even munched on coffee beans. I wanted weighty foods, something that would not just fill my stomach but stretch it to its limits, make me feel like I would burst. I felt possessed by an evil alter ego wolfing down a loaf of bread straight out of the plastic, an entire bag of carrots to the point of turning orange, or a whole watermelon the size of a full-term belly. I knew I was in trouble when I opened a box of cereal because I couldn't stop once I started.

Sometimes I would throw up involuntarily because my stomach simply couldn't take it. Other times when I got started on more calorific foods, I would set out to throw up afterwards, the way I used to at my boarding school in Korea. The other strategy I adopted was to chew and spit into a plastic bag, as if into a spit bucket at a wine tasting, to avoid swallowing and thus consuming calories.

In many ways, I was more ashamed of my binge-eating than my drinking because it made me feel like a greedy child who couldn't control her food intake. Alcohol only made it worse by disinhibiting any sense of self-control. After drinking, I would succumb to my late-night cravings, like for the Singaporean fried noodles from the local Chinese takeaway, ironically called Double Happy.

At the same time, my binge-eating had the strange

effect of comforting me, that maybe my problem wasn't alcoholism per se but a more generic addictive behavior. It just so happened that alcohol was one of my addictions. That sounded less damning than being an alcoholic, right? There was just so much shame and stigma attached to the A word. I knew people who suffered from depression but not a single alcoholic. I wondered if any of my colleagues were silently suffering too. Maybe they, too, were good at hiding it.

Or maybe drinking was a symptom of my depression, which was the *real* problem. It was more convenient for me to believe that I was drinking because I was depressed, and not the other way around, because drinking felt so inevitable. Alcohol was my lifeline.

Maybe it was about control. A misplaced need for it, whether through alcohol, food or even routine. I felt like I was exercising extreme self-control during the day, just by not exploding or breaking down at work, that I needed something to help me switch off, let go, escape into oblivion. I also felt as if I had no control over any aspect of my life except my own body. Besides, it wasn't like I was using cocaine or heroin, or harming anyone (but myself). It was "just" alcohol and food. Ironically, I would prove I was in control by drinking and eating uncontrollably: I could do what I liked with my body.

But whether I made it out to be about depression, a need for control or general addiction, the truth was, I was chemically dependent on alcohol. I drank regardless, whether it was a good day or a bad day, whether I was alone or in company. Because I needed it.

I wanted to quit my job so badly. When I was feeling very depressed, the partner who led my team let me take time off as sick leave to focus on my well-being. Penny knew I was biding my time—five years—to gain permanent residence in the UK. In fact, I handed in my resignation twice, but she talked me out of it both times and advised me to stay on. As an Australian who had been naturalized herself, Penny knew how important it would be for me to secure my right to live in the UK without a visa. I knew Penny had never been depressed before—she told me this—but I could tell she was trying to be understanding.

With each day I made it through, the opportunity cost became higher. It was the classic sunk cost fallacy: all that time I spent miserable, it couldn't have been for nothing.

Even if I quit, what would I do? Where would I go? I remembered how depressed I was job hunting in Korea, how difficult it was to get visa sponsorship, how happy I was to be offered this role. I couldn't return to Korea, tail between my legs. Besides, I had no confidence that I would find happiness elsewhere.

28

Of all the times I wanted to kill myself, I never imagined I would come closest on my graduation day. Back when all my friends were posting their graduation photos on Facebook, I had to get my bachelor's degree in absentia as I had already returned to Korea. Luckily, Oxford has a system whereby, seven years after you matriculate for your bachelor's, you are conferred a master's purely by the passage of time, another one of those elitist Oxbridge practices dating back to the Middle Ages. For me, it was another opportunity to have a degree ceremony, a picture-perfect day with mortarboards thrown high as proud parents take one more photo to make the moment last.

I started planning months ahead. Not only had I not seen my parents in a while, but my dad hadn't had the chance to visit Oxford while I was a student. In fact, he had only been once in the late eighties as a tourist. I hoped visiting as the parent of an Oxford graduate would be far more gratifying. He wouldn't be among the throngs of Asian tourists denied entry to university sites, but with his own daughter who had come top of her class. Hopefully he would see that the £30,000 tuition fee he had surrendered each year was worth it. I booked hotels and train tickets and three restaurants, just in case, well in advance.

After some months full of anticipation, my parents arrived from Paris on the Eurostar the evening before the ceremony. (I'm not sure where my brother was. By this time, he had retired as a professional esports player and become a coach for the same game, *Dota 2*. His team was based in Utrecht in the Netherlands, but they traveled frequently for competitions and it didn't even occur to me that he would attend my graduation. I hadn't seen or spoken to him in years.)

The next morning, I picked up my parents from the hotel I'd booked for them next to my flat in Canary Wharf. So far, so good, all in line with the detailed itinerary I had emailed them of the three days they would be spending here: *8:15 a.m. leave hotel, take Tube to Paddington. Breakfast not included; buy at train station.*

When we arrived at my college in Oxford, I was anxious to see my dad's expression as he saw where I had lived and studied for three years. I showed him around, pointing excitedly at the Beehive. "This was my first-year room," I said. My dad's reaction was disappointingly muted.

There was a briefing meeting for graduates that I had to attend, so I suggested my parents roam the college grounds while they waited. I directed them to Canterbury Quad, where the impressive college library was located. "How was it?" I asked, after the briefing. But again, he just shrugged.

As we entered the beautiful Hall for lunch, though, my dad seemed to look up in awe at the high ceilings and imposing portraits. I spotted our name cards along the long rows of tables. My mom and I sat with our backs against the wood-paneled walls and my dad across from us, inspecting the St John's placemat and cutlery. We shared a polite smile with the families on either side. Then everyone stood for grace, spoken in Latin. I loved that my dad was getting a taste of the Oxford experience.

Staff came around asking, "Red or white?" My dad went for white, and I asked for some red. As the food started to be served from the far end of the table, my dad craned his neck to see what was on the menu. It looked delicious, a hearty portion of salmon. But when it came to our turn and the staff extended a plate over my dad's shoulder, he mumbled in Korean, "Is salmon all you got? I could really have done with some steak."

"Pardon?" she said.

I jumped over the table. "Oh no, it's nothing, sorry," I said, trying not to frown. I didn't know why my dad was being difficult—he loves salmon—but I didn't want to create a scene.

As we finished our mains, the staff came around to replenish our glasses. My dad looked approvingly as his was refilled with more white wine. I hoped that would put him in a better mood. After dessert, I gave my parents directions to the Sheldonian Theatre, where the ceremony was going to be held, as I would be making my way separately with the rest of the graduates.

I sat in my designated seat at this historic site, a D-shaped building designed by Sir Christopher Wren, and was soon joined by Paul, who had booked his ceremony to coincide with mine even though we weren't together. As the theater filled up, we eyed the rows of benches above us and waved at our families.

The ceremony started ostentatiously with the Pro-Vice-Chancellor entering, preceded by the Bedels and followed by the Proctors and Registrar, all dressed in their elaborate gowns. The proceedings were conducted in Latin, as if we were in the twelfth century. I was surprised to recognize my anthropology tutor on stage, speaking in Latin beautifully. Next to him was an older woman who had clearly never spoken any Latin before and had been brought in to substitute. She stumbled her way through the passages, her rising intonation at the end of each word betraying how clueless she was. I felt for the poor lady, though she could have feigned confidence. It wasn't like anyone in the audience understood what she was saying.

The degrees were conferred in order, starting with the oldest and highest, so it was a long wait before our turn. Paul and I whispered silly jokes to each other as we watched all the doctorates and degrees in medicine go first. Finally, it was the Master of Arts. When my name was called out, I said, "*Do fidem*" (I swear), as briefed, and shook the hands of a few important-looking people on stage. It felt like I was in a play. There was even a costume change "backstage," in another building, where we had to quickly change out of our bachelor's and into our master's gowns and hoods.

Once the ceremony was over, Paul and I split up to look for our families among all the parents, grandparents, siblings and other halves spilling out of the theater. I found my parents and skipped over with a big, expectant grin.

The first thing my dad said to me was, "Man, it looks like even dogs and cows can get a doctorate these days." Dogs and cows: a Korean expression whose literal translation seems to convey the meaning accurately. Yes, the ceremony was long, but couldn't he have just said "Congratulations"? Was that really too much to ask? I winced but said nothing.

Meanwhile, Paul had found his family and came over to say hello. My mom and his father had met before, but we made the introduction for the others and everyone exchanged some pleasantries, my mom complimenting Paul's grandmother on her youthful appearance. I sensed, however, that my dad was not keen to mingle, so after taking a quick group photo, we wished each other a good rest of the day.

"C'mon, let's get going now," my dad said tetchily as soon as they were out of earshot.

My mom and I exchanged confused looks.

"I want to change out of my suit," he demanded.

"We haven't even taken photos yet," I said to my mom. But my dad was already trailing off. I couldn't understand why he needed to change right that minute.

"Lena wants to take a few more photos," my mom said in a conciliatory tone.

"What for?" was the response.

My mom could see how upset I was, and how unreasonable my dad was being, but she also knew she could not be seen to be taking sides so as not to undermine his authority. "Let your dad go off first. Why don't we stay back and take some photos?" she said, sounding like she was mediating a kids' fight.

"It's fine, let's just go," I said. It was too late, my face was already strained, my eyes watery.

"Come on, just you and me," she tried again.

"No, I said it's fine." I was reminded of my dance recital in the US when the first thing my dad said to me at the end was, "What are we waiting for? Let's go now." It was no different this time around.

As we left the Sheldonian, I told my mom we needed to stop by my college to pick up my graduation certificate. She passed on the message to my dad, who was marching off ahead of us.

"What do you want that scrap of paper for?" he scoffed.

My mom and I exchanged looks, unable to say anything. If my certificate was not worth the five minutes' walk to college, we at least needed to collect the bottle of champagne I had asked the porters to keep chilled for us so we could celebrate in a park straight after the ceremony. So we traipsed back to college, now me first, my mom a few steps back, and my dad farther back still. I forced a smile as I collected my certificate and the bottle of champagne from the porters. On our walk back to the B&B we had booked for the night, we stopped by the store I had hired my graduation gowns from.

"Are you sure you don't want to keep them until tomorrow morning?" my mom asked.

"No, I said it's fine."

When we arrived in our room, my dad took off his tie and changed out of his suit. *There, you got what you wanted. Happy now?* I thought. Still, I hoped to salvage the day. We took the champagne and some glasses from the B&B and found a patch to sit on in the Christ Church Meadow. My dad popped open the bottle and I desperately hoped the champagne would diffuse the tension. It was the one thing my dad and I could count on: my mom hated bubbles, so he welcomed any opportunity to share a bottle with me. We commented on the apple-y taste of the champagne. After a glass, he tried to make some small talk, but that disgusted me even more.

Then a few raindrops hurried us to dinner. We trailed along the Thames to the restaurant I had reserved months before. It had a lovely atmosphere, like a Scandinavian café, decorated tastefully with birdcages and fairy lights. We were shown to our table, which was right in the middle of an elongated area. There were other diners: a few couples and a big group of families with two graduates still in their degree gowns.

My mom and dad sat across from each other, and I sat next to my mom with an empty seat in front of me. We browsed the menu and discussed what to order. No one was hungry, so we decided to share two starters and two mains, including a steak. For drinks, I suggested we ask to taste two wines before ordering.

"Just order anything," my dad said. "There's not one drinkable bottle here."

"What's your problem?" I said.

After our order was taken, my mom and I tried to make some small talk. I forget what about, but it felt stilted trying to fill the awkward silence. My dad sat there stiffly, excluded from the conversation. He'd always had a vertical crease etched into the middle of his forehead—it seemed to be deepening now.

"You can't speak to your father like that," he said as soon as our starters were served.

"What?" I glared at him, then at my mom, then back at him. I tried to explain myself through gritted teeth. "Do you have any idea—"

"I have never been abusive! Did I ever hit you once?"

What the fuck was he talking about? Hot tears started streaming down my cheeks. I could feel my blood pressure rising from my throat to the tip of my head, like in a cartoon. Unable to express myself in words, I gripped my knife tighter and tighter. "*This* is what you make me want to do," I spat, as I simulated slitting my throat, before immediately being taken aback by my own behavior.

My dad gave a nervous laughter. "Gosh, you're just like my younger brother when you do that." I had no idea what he was talking about.

As I sat there still clasping my knife, he continued, "You can't treat me this way. You must respect me!" I was dumbstruck by his comments, then seething.

My mom tried to diffuse the situation. "What Lena's trying to say is…" She looked at me, but I couldn't see clearly anymore, my eyes glazed with tears. "Come on, let's get some fresh air," she said.

"It's fine. Let's just eat," I managed.

But then my breathing started getting heavier and heavier. I couldn't take it anymore. I got up, put my jacket on and headed out of the restaurant. At the exit, I turned around and looking straight at my dad, shouted as loud as I could, "FUUUUCKKKKK YOUUU!!!!!!!!!" It must have rung across the whole of Oxford. Everyone in the restaurant stared at me, flabbergasted.

As I turned to leave, two girls sitting outside the restaurant glanced at each other and giggled. "What the fuck?"

I stormed up St Aldate's towards the B&B as fast as I could, hyperventilating the whole time, each inhalation like a drowning person gasping for air. I tried to impose a rhythm on my breath but it was outside my control.

My mom came running after me. "Lena, please, I'm so sorry, please calm down, let's go back inside."

"Get away from me," I said. She tried to keep pace with me for a bit but then returned to the restaurant after confirming I was headed to the B&B. I must have looked psychotic, tramping and hyperventilating loudly all the way down the High Street.

When I got to the B&B, I asked the lady at reception for the key to our room and a cab, immediately. I hurriedly packed my backpack so I could get the hell out of there but was soon joined by my mom. I don't know how she followed me so fast but she kept repeating how sorry she was and pleaded with me to calm down. I bawled at her in Korean, "I told you to fuck off. FUCKKKK OFFFF!!!!!" I had never sworn at her before. She asked me where I was headed now, so I told her I was going back to London.

I got the cab to the train station and bought a familiar bottle of Pinot Noir from the Marks & Spencer. I contemplated killing myself in the public toilets but decided to wait until I got home. I wasn't ready. I needed more wine.

The carriage was mostly empty except for a group of two girls and two boys facing each other right in front of me. They chattered away, politely pretending they couldn't see me in tears, sipping wine out of a plastic cup. I could at least breathe again by this point. I wondered what they made of me. Had I been dumped by a boyfriend? Did a grandparent die? I bet they couldn't have guessed that it was my graduation day, and I was on my way home to kill myself.

I drafted a stream-of-consciousness text for my mom (in Korean):

It's not your fault. You are the biggest victim in all this. No one is born because they want to be, but I'm someone who really shouldn't have been. I felt that since I was ten or so in Malaysia. I wanted to jump from the apartment. There were many other instances. […] I've wanted to die many times since, for reasons unrelated to him. In that sense, I kind of feel grateful to him. You're such a kind and lovely person. What was your luck in all this? You are the biggest tragedy. You didn't do anything wrong. But maybe that's life. 99 percent of things are outside your control. I feel so bad for you. I'm so similar to him in personality, but you are such a good person. What a tragedy. But no one decides their own fate. […] Life is so predictable and tedious. I didn't want to go through life anyway. I feel weird, but also free. I know this is the right thing to do.

I pressed send.

I needed to do this. I needed him to know: You made me kill myself. No, you killed your daughter. How else would he understand? How else was he going to learn? I googled "how to tie a noose" and the results showed suicide helplines. I scrolled down and clicked on a ten-step wikiHow guide, with pictures, apparently meant for Halloween decorations or for fishing and boating purposes. I cried at the shock my

216

mom would feel when she came to see her daughter hanging off the back of a door.

I ordered an Uber to Paddington station. I remember chatting to the driver, though I can't remember what about. I wondered if he would ever find out that my conversation with him was my last ever in this realm.

I felt clearheaded when I was dropped off outside my flat in Canary Wharf. This was the only logical conclusion to the night. All I needed was courage, so I drank some more. That would numb the pain. I wanted this to be quick and unpainful. I wanted it to be over.

I looked nostalgically at the fluffy baby blue bathrobe hanging in my room. I used to wear this so frequently my mom called it my "uniform." I strung off the soft belt and tied it around my neck, like putting a leash on a dog. I couldn't remember the step-by-step instructions on the wikiHow page but figured a double knot would do. I tied the other end to the coat hook on my door. I could still stand on my feet, but I'd read that that was alright as long as you let your feet drop. The second I did, my throat choked tight. I managed two seconds before I was back on my feet. *Don't be such a wimp*, I told myself and tried again. This time for five seconds. My face flushed bright red. This would be nowhere near enough. I texted my mom: "It's not so easy to die."

I needed more alcohol and a change of strategy. I went to the shared kitchen and grabbed my chef's knife. Back in my room, I rested the sharp blade on my wrist, but the touch of cold metal sobered me up straight. I couldn't do it. I put the knife aside and hated myself for my inability to execute. This wouldn't do either.

I started rummaging through my drawers for all the medication I could find. There was a big Ziploc full of emergency medicine my mom had packed for me when I'd left Korea three years earlier. They each had a sticky label in my mom's handwriting—how many to take and when. I didn't touch those. There was some ibuprofen and paracetamol and painkillers I had bought to treat an infection following a wisdom tooth removal a few months earlier. They were effervescent tablets for immediate pain relief. I hoped these would now relieve me of my pain forever. I dissolved all the fizzy tablets I could find in a cup of water, seven or eight of them, and used the murky potion to down as many tablets of ibuprofen and paracetamol as I could. Then I lay on my bed and closed my eyes.

∽

Damn it. I had failed. I was still here. I scrambled to the bathroom clutching at my chest and vomited a cloudy liquid tasting of codeine. I had barely eaten anything since the lunch at college, so was retching up whatever liquid was lingering in my stomach. Then I started sweating profusely. Had I not taken enough drugs? This must be why overdosing was an ineffective method of suicide.

I threw away the packaging of all the drugs I'd torn open and returned the knife to the kitchen. There was something surreal about this situation. I wondered what my parents were up to. Were they having an English breakfast at the B&B? What happened yesterday? Did my dad eat the steak?

My mom messaged late in the morning to say she would

come by to pick up a large trunk she was supposed to take back to Paris. I asked her to bring me some beef pho from the food truck outside the Tube stop. The arrangement was that I would leave the trunk outside the flat and she would leave my soup there. But she knocked when she came. I tried to ignore her but she begged to come in. She'd also bought herself a bowl and wanted to eat it with me. She said we didn't have to talk; she just wanted a place to eat. I refused, and she left. Then it started raining and I felt bad, so I messaged for her to come back. We ate in my room, in silence. She left, not noticing anything wrong with me. I remember thinking it odd given the content of the messages I had sent her the night before.

After she left, I lay in bed all day, and the following two days, which I'd already taken off work to spend with my parents. Out of boredom, I looked up the symptoms of overdosing. The Wikipedia page on paracetamol poisoning stated: "Most people have few or non-specific symptoms in the first 24 hours following overdose. This is typically followed by a couple of days without any symptoms after which yellowish skin, blood clotting problems, and confusion occurs. Additional complications may include kidney failure, pancreatitis, low blood sugar, and lactic acidosis. Without treatment some cases will resolve while others will result in death."

I was suddenly terrified. Was I slowly dying? I wanted to be dead, not die a slow death with all these alarming complications. I called Paul and asked him to come to me straight away. I told him what had happened since we parted ways outside the Sheldonian and showed him the Wikipedia page. He said I needed to go to the hospital immediately.

I went to A&E and waited skittishly after filling out some forms. I felt guilty claiming I had an emergency when I looked completely fine, but my reality could have been worse than someone rushing in with a broken bone or gushing blood. I was called into a curtained room and a man, I'm not sure if he was a nurse or a doctor, asked me exactly what I had consumed. I spoke quietly, conscious that people could hear me through the curtains.

Paul arrived shortly after, and we waited for my blood test results in a private room. "What would you do if they told me I had three days left?" I asked, trying to sound lighthearted, but I was scared. According to Wikipedia, the damage was irreversible if I was on the path for liver failure.

A nurse entered an hour later with an update. She said my first sample had coagulated and so she would need to take my blood again. Despite her reassurance that this kind of thing happened occasionally, I was convinced that I was dying and they wanted to make sure before delivering the verdict. Another hour and a half after my second blood test, a young doctor came in and told me my results were fine. However, she'd have to do a mental health assessment of whether I was at risk. I replied to her questions frivolously, smiling and trying to make light of the situation. We were dismissed at 1 a.m.

~

The following days, all I could think was: What was wrong with him? The salmon. My dad likes salmon. Why did he need to make such a fuss? Then his snide comments following the ceremony—the "dogs and cows" getting doctorates, my graduate certificate which was but a "scrap of paper"—his obstinate demand to change out of his suit, then all that stuff he said at the restaurant.

Draining as it was to have to relive the day, I told some of my close friends what had happened. I needed an explanation, some validation, an objective assessment by a third party. One friend observed, "He sounds like someone who's jealous." *Jealous?!* I'd never heard that before, a parent being jealous of their child. Shouldn't he be proud? But the constant need to be dismissive, to put me down, that was a hallmark of jealousy. He *was* jealous. Perhaps he was envious of the upbringing I'd had, everything handed to me on a plate as far as he could see.

Maybe he also felt competitive. Something like, "You think salmon is a treat? I am the ambassador and am far better catered to." Maybe he wanted to ground me and reaffirm his superiority. He always wanted me to show him respect—that was his big thing.

Perhaps it was more fundamental, a cultural and generational difference in our expectations of the father role. *I have never been abusive! Did I ever hit you once?* He was right. My dad was never physically abusive, he never cheated on my mom, and he always provided a roof over our heads. By those standards, he had been a great father.

These "explanations" for my dad's behavior, however, did little to quell my anger and contempt for him. He had not only ruined my graduation day but poisoned my entire Oxford experience, which had been three of the most enriching years of my life. I never wanted to go back now. The way I saw it, he had almost taken away my life too. I could never forgive him.

Three months after my graduation, my dad turned sixty. Traditionally, sixty years marks one full cycle of life through the twelve animals of the zodiac, multiplied by the five natural elements: wood, fire, earth, metal and water. It's the most important birthday after your first *dol* celebration. But all I could feel on my dad's sixtieth birthday was disgust. Time was supposed to heal, but this was going to take much longer.

I wanted to erase all memory of that day but couldn't stop reenacting the scenes in my head, wondering what was wrong with my dad, why he acted the way he did, the whole time taking it for granted that anyone would want to kill themselves under the circumstances. It took many more months before I started to wonder beyond why my dad acted the way he did and instead why I reacted the way I did. How had I come to think that killing myself was the solution?

29

Although everything exploded on my graduation day and my dad was the ostensible trigger, the truth was I'd been suffering from depression and alcoholism throughout my twenties. Well, the problems started much earlier. I stuck my head out our fifteenth-floor apartment and wrote "I'd like to suicide" in my diary when I was only ten. I started binge-drinking to oblivion when I was thirteen. I was bulimic when I was fifteen. The thought of death was ever-present in my head. Why? Was I born this way?

At the back of my mind, and for some time now, I'd had a nagging suspicion that all the moving around had something to do with my mental health problems. But I couldn't articulate how. Besides, I was supposed to feel gratitude—"always be grateful to your admirable parents who have given you this opportunity" is what my third-grade teacher had said.

What people saw was our glamorous lifestyle: all the countries we've lived in, the places we've traveled to, the languages we speak. They imagine how luxurious it would be to have a chef, a cleaner and a driver. They see the benefits and privileges of a global upbringing, not the difficulties and challenges, and certainly not the idea that such privilege might lead to serious mental health issues.

It was in utter desperation for answers that I tried googling: frequent moves during childhood; moving countries as a child; can moving make you depressed?

The results left me speechless.

A study published in the *Journal of Personality and Social Psychology* followed over 7,000 American adults for ten years and found that frequent relocations in childhood were related to poorer well-being in adulthood (Oishi & Schimmack 2010). Introverts who had moved frequently as children were more likely to have died during the ten-year follow-up. That was me, a clear introvert, though one masquerading as an extrovert by necessity.

Another study published in the *American Journal of Preventive Medicine* tracked every single person born in Denmark between 1971 and 1997—1.4 million people—and found that people who lived in various places growing up had an increased risk of suicide, substance misuse and even early death (Webb, Pedersen & Mok 2016). The more frequent the move, the more likely to have adverse health outcomes later in life. In other words, each additional move was associated with an incremental increase in risk. What did that mean for me? I moved every three years of my life—that's seven international moves by the time I went to university.

The researchers also found that the older the children were when they moved, the more likely they were to attempt suicide. A child who goes through a residential move at age fourteen has double the risk of suicide by middle age. Let me repeat that: *A child who goes through a residential move at age fourteen has double the risk of suicide by middle age.* Age fourteen is exactly when I moved from the US to Korea.

It was a strange feeling. On the one hand, I felt relieved. Maybe I wasn't born this way. But on the other hand, I still felt doomed. I couldn't change my past, so what now? The damage was done. I emailed the articles to my mom with no subject or message, just the attachments, silently accusatory.

But then something shifted. I stopped wondering what was wrong with me and instead thought, *No wonder.* No wonder I struggle to connect with anyone, no wonder I feel no sense of control over my life, no wonder I'm depressed. Reading the articles gave me the validation I needed to feel like I wasn't just being self-indulgent, wallowing in self-pity, but that I had a point. I could stop being so apologetic about my privilege, afraid of sounding like a brat—a "diplobrat" as we are sometimes called. What I was going through was real.

Growing up, everything changed every three years: not only my house, school and friends but the language, the food, the culture, the climate, the color of people's skin, the contour of their faces, the expressions and body language, the way people made eye contact (or didn't), the food portions, the clothing sizes, what was considered skinny or fat, polite or impolite, rich or poor, normal or abnormal. Everything changed. And with it, inevitably, me.

The word "identity" comes from the Latin *idem*, meaning "same." But you can't stay the same, unmoving, unchanged when the world around you is changing, radically, drastically. As my world swung between East and West, back and forth, my whole identity swung in tandem, like a pendulum. One day I was an effortless all-A student, and the next at the bottom of my class, a rotten apple that parents didn't want their kids associating with. Then once more, I was magically transformed into the teacher's pet with perfect grades again. One day my family could afford a comfortable expat life, and the next, I resented feeling "poor" as a young teen trying to fit in to a wealthy suburb. Later, I would live in the official residence with chandeliers and a literal red carpet, but then struggle my way through successive flatshares in London. One day I was doing everything to disown my Koreanness, and the next, I was a "banana" surrounded by nothing but Koreans. No wonder I had a disjointed sense of self.

As I dug further, I came across the concept of unresolved grief among highly mobile people like me. At first, I winced. Grief sounded melodramatic. No one had died. But then I started to recognize the many significant losses and abrupt endings in my life that I hadn't come to terms with, even all these years later. Nearly two decades ago, Mary had written to me:

Lena, I don't know how im going to say goodbye to u knowing that im probably never going to see you again. Saying goodbye to you will be like taking part of my life away from me in a matter of seconds. I love you so much lena and thank you so much for moving here, coming into my life, and spending all this time together with me. I LOVE YOU LENA I SERIOUSLY WILL NEVER FORGET YOU...

The tone might sound melodramatic, but the loss was real. Mary had added at the bottom, "never get rid of this..."

And I didn't. We still haven't seen each other again, but I spoke to her recently on FaceTime and she really hasn't changed one bit.

Prior to publishing this book, I also reached out to my first love, Yoonhak, to ask his permission to share our story. We hadn't spoken in over a decade, so I had no idea how he would react. Within minutes of seeing him on video, though, I was in tears. The emotions were raw, for both of us, as if we'd been transported back to high school. I felt so confused afterwards: I was in my thirties now, so what was I doing crying about a boy from when I was sixteen? This was unresolved grief.

Growing up, none of my friendships lasted over three years. Three years was their shelf life. After that, with one flight, I'd be on the other side of the world, trying to make new friends. This cycle repeated many times over had had a profound effect on the way I approached relationships. A rare study of *international* relocations—American adolescents studying in Europe and Taiwan—reported that "*such teenagers, by the nature of their overseas experience, become more isolated, develop fewer friends, have a less positive view of themselves and of the future but at the same time become more self-reliant and individualistic. They find themselves unable and unwilling to invest in close, long-term relationships because they recognize that such relationships are either impossible to sustain or painful to end*" (Werkman et al. 1981). No wonder I didn't believe in friendships. No wonder I'd become more isolated and individualistic.

I started to recognize the various stages of grief I was stuck in—denial, anger, bargaining, depression. I often found myself wondering, *What if I hadn't moved around so much? What if I hadn't gone to Myongji? What if, what if?* I needed to grant myself permission to grieve, to mourn my losses so that one day I could reach the final stage: acceptance.

Once I started seeing my upbringing in this new light, everything changed. I couldn't change my past, but it all started to click, as if my brain was being rewired. This click in my brain—without any alcohol involved—gave me the confidence I needed to quit drinking.

~

The previous times I'd tried to quit, my sobriety lasted no more than a few weeks. For a long time, I'd wondered whether I had a genetic predisposition to alcoholism, maybe from my grandpa. I wondered if my wanting to get drunk faster than my friends even at the age of thirteen was the earliest manifestation of it. But now, with this newfound understanding, I felt like I could do it.

I went to the local library and browsed the self-help section. After swiftly checking out a few promising titles, I went home and started with the self-assessment: *How often do you have a drink containing alcohol?* The highest frequency. *How many units of alcohol do you drink on a typical day?* The highest number. *How often were you not able to stop drinking once you started?* Almost always. *How often have you felt guilt or remorse after drinking?* Almost always. I needed to quit if only because my ego could not tolerate the intense shame I felt reading self-help books for alcoholics. I didn't want to end up in AA meetings.

The first week was not easy. I showed all the typical withdrawal symptoms, feeling constantly dizzy and nauseous, almost worse than if I'd been hungover. I felt ravenous after big meals and my brain yearned for that feeling of neurons clicking into place. I'd clearly become chemically dependent.

Without alcohol to keep me company, I was feeling restless in the evenings and needed something to pass the time, so two days after I quit, I signed up to a twenty-day introductory offer at a hot yoga studio around the corner from my office. At first, I struggled with the forty-degree heat and felt queasy bending backwards and forwards. I thought I might have joined some weird cult participating in the deep breathing exercises at the beginning and end of class. But there was something about the heat that allowed me to lose myself totally. I had to channel all my attention and physical energy to kick my leg back in the standing bow pose or to hold the trikonasana triangle pose. I never felt more clearheaded than during those ninety minutes and I felt cleansed coming out drenched in sweat. I also liked the discipline of holding the same twenty-six poses again and again and kept going back.

As I counted each day of sobriety, the days became weeks, and the weeks became months. I loved waking up without a hangover. I slept better, I lost weight, my skin glowed. Colleagues remarked on how happy I looked. I felt better than ever.

Then I met my boyfriend, Henry.

I'd known Henry for a few years. He worked in a different team on the same floor and sometimes we'd grab lunch together with a mutual work friend, though I hadn't really noticed him. Then, somewhere along the line, I started looking forward to these lunches. I started wearing heels and dressing nicely to work. I took advantage of the office's hot-desking policy to reserve seats that were closer to his team, never mind they were not with my own.

Henry seemed somewhat flirtatious with me but in the most reserved way. He didn't wear a wedding band and never seemed to say "we" when talking about his personal life, but he was also quite private and I couldn't figure out a subtle way to ask if he had a girlfriend. I decided to take a chance and invited him to come to hot yoga with me after work one day. He pretended to relent only because I was being insistent, but I took it as a clear sign he was interested in me. If not, I would make sure he was by the end of class: my yoga costume was but a sports bra and a pair of Lycra booty shorts.

Henry did surprisingly well for his first class, trying his best to do all the postures in the heat. I could see him behind me in the mirror, though I tried not to stare—drenched in sweat, Henry's shirt and shorts stuck to him tight. The next day in the office, he teased that I might have been more flexible but that his balance was better—I wobbled around doing the eagle pose. It seemed clear he was flirting with me now.

Henry kept joining me at yoga after work once or twice a week and even cycled in one Sunday. It was his birthday the following day, so after class I gave him a T-shirt that said "yogi" on it. Cute and flirtatious, I thought. When he opened the gift, his face flushed bright red, even redder than it already was from class, which made me flush in turn. Since he'd come all this way, I mustered the courage to ask him out for a drink, but he came up with some lame excuse to go home.

The next day at work, I decided to ping him on the work messaging app: "I think you owe me an explanation."

It must have been obvious to him, and frankly the entire floor, that I was throwing myself at him. Over my shoulder, I could see he was at his desk and had his chat window open. To help him out, I sent another message: "Are you gay?" My friends would later tease me that it's awfully confident of me to assume homosexuality would be the only reason a guy isn't interested in me, but I could see no other explanation at the time.

After what seemed like an eternity, Henry replied: "No, I am not…"

"Then what?" I asked.

I could tell he was typing, then deleting, then typing again. Finally: "I'm flattered, but not interested."

Excuse me, you're flattered, but not interested?

Henry asked if I wanted to chat in person, so we went to the canteen, which was empty at this time of the afternoon. Sitting across from each other in one of the booths, we waited for the other person to speak first.

"I'm sorry if I've done anything to lead you on," he said at last.

Lead me on? As if going to hot yoga with a colleague was a normal after-work activity?

"I've just never thought of you that way," he added.

Since I'd established he wasn't gay, my first thought was maybe he's racist. Or just not into Asian girls. But I couldn't say that to him, so I just looked down at my hands and fidgeted. I'd been on many Tinder dates but Henry was the first guy I actually liked since Paul, and I really liked him a lot. And I was so sure he liked me back.

Henry asked if I still wanted to be friends and I said yes, just so I didn't have to avoid him at work. To distract myself, I went on some dates with a tall, dark, handsome Brazilian guy I met on Tinder. Meanwhile, Henry continued to come to hot yoga with me. Talk about mixed messages.

A few weeks later, the office chat was all about Christmas plans: where everyone was going, whose side of the family, how many presents they needed to buy. I didn't have any plans. I would be right at my flat three minutes from the office, probably with my landlady Simona, who didn't have any plans either.

Then Henry messaged me one evening and invited me to spend Christmas Day with his family.

"Really? Are you sure?" I said, my heart fluttering. Now I was really confused. Had he changed his mind about me? Or did he just feel sorry for me? Or maybe he was jealous? I had mentioned the hot Brazilian guy to him just to act cool given I'd been rejected.

"Yes, it'll just be my mum and sister this year, but you should come."

Whatever his reasons, I said I'd be delighted to. I asked him what his mom was like, trying not to think of her as my potential future mother-in-law. Henry reassured me I didn't have to worry about anything and wrote her address on a Post-it note for me.

I'd never been so nervous going to someone's house. Henry didn't tell me a dress code, so I wasn't sure how smart or casual to dress. After trying on every outfit, I decided on a beige top and matching leather skirt. I wore some pearl earrings and did my hair half-up, half-down. Holding a bottle of champagne and some macaroons, I rang the doorbell in the late afternoon, timing my arrival for just after the Queen's speech as Henry had suggested. Henry opened the door and leaned in to kiss me on each cheek. He introduced me to his mother, Anna, an elegant but energetic woman in her late sixties, and his sister, Rachel, who was tall and lovely and in her late thirties. They were both so warm and welcoming I knew I had nothing to worry about as soon as I met them, though I wondered how Henry had described me to them: as a colleague, a yoga buddy, or someone who had a crush on him?

Anna's house was decorated beautifully with paintings, lamps and antique furniture. There were perfectly curated piles of home and gardening magazines and family photos displayed on a round mahogany table. It felt homely. Henry, Anna and Rachel were all super-attentive, making sure I felt comfortable as we chatted in the living area. They spoke so politely and sweetly, not just to me but to each other. Henry called his mother "mummy" and she called him "sweetie." It seemed too sweet, like something out of a children's book. I wondered if they were putting it on for me. I couldn't imagine my own family speaking like that.

"Shall we do presents?" Anna suggested. I had only brought a small something for Henry, a book called *Quiet*:

The Power of Introverts in a World That Can't Stop Talking by Susan Cain. I had read it that summer and found it revolutionary. Instead of writing him a card, which I worried might be too formal, I stuck a sticky note on the first page with a simple message—"Merry Christmas!"—but I turned the dot on the exclamation mark into a small heart. Henry smiled bashfully as he read my note and mouthed, "Thank you." I smiled back, trying to ignore Anna and Rachel exchanging a cheeky glance. I wasn't expecting anything in return, but Henry had gotten me a psychedelic blue lululemon water bottle that would keep my water cold at hot yoga. It was very sweet.

Henry, Anna and Rachel exclaimed in delight as they opened each other's presents and kissed each other on the cheeks. "Thank you, Henry, this is so thoughtful of you. It's exactly what I wanted," Rachel would say. Anna and Rachel had prepared presents for me too, so I wouldn't feel left out. They got me a shower gift set and a soap set and apologized for not coordinating between themselves before. "You really didn't have to get me anything," I said, genuinely touched.

After opening presents, we moved to the dining area. Anna had prepared an exquisite Christmas meal with all the trimmings, though she kept apologizing that she had gotten the timings wrong. Everything looked perfect to me. Once Henry did the honors with the turkey, we served ourselves—I wished I didn't have to go first but they insisted I was the guest. As instructed, I sat across from Anna.

"Henry, sweetie, would you open the champagne for us?" Anna asked.

Pop! Henry offered me the first drink and I accepted it

nonchalantly. I hadn't drunk for over four months, but I'd already decided I would have a drink that day. We clinked our glasses, and I took my first sip. It was uneventful. None of the clicking of the neurons that I used to be desperate for. I was going to be okay.

The conversation centered on my global upbringing. Anna was fascinated and had endless questions for me. I mostly made eye contact with her out of respect, but I knew Henry was as engrossed. He was hearing it all for the first time too. Anna asked me what Christmas was like in Korea and what my family was up to. I felt lame telling her, "Nothing, really." Christmas Day was a public holiday, but there was no real tradition to speak of. Most people celebrated it with friends or on dates.

For dessert, we had a slice of the Christmas cake Anna had baked. "You have to have it with the icing," she said. It was fruitcake with everything I didn't like, raisins and rum, but I helped myself to show my appreciation.

At one point during the evening, Anna recounted her bemusement when Henry asked to invite a "colleague" over for Christmas, especially when that colleague was female. "He's never suggested anything like that before," she said, "but I told Henry he can bring in all the waifs and strays." She gave a hearty laugh and added, "No one should be spending Christmas alone."

I flinched. I knew "waifs and strays" was just an expression and all she meant was that all were welcome, but I suddenly felt defensive. I was not a waif or a stray. I had a loving mother and maybe not a loving father, but a father who loved me. They just happened to be in Korea. I really missed them in that moment.

At the same time, I'd never had a Christmas like that.

Two days later, Henry came to hot yoga, and I knew it was different as soon as I saw him. When we lay down in savasana in between poses, I could feel his breath on my body and the electrical currents flowing from the tip of his fingers to mine. I so wanted to grab his hand.

After class, Henry finally made a move and kissed me. It was our first "date," but we were already talking about whether we wanted children.

(Needless to say, Henry stopped coming to hot yoga once we were together. And yet he still claims he was purely interested in improving his flexibility and balance at the time.)

30

A few months later, I was in Stockholm visiting my friend Tyra, who had studied Human Sciences in the year below me at Oxford. I learned through my mom that my brother also happened to be in Stockholm that same week for an esports competition. It was such a coincidence we couldn't not arrange to meet up.

But then I couldn't bear to think of the awkwardness of having a whole meal with my brother, one-on-one. What would we say to each other? I hadn't seen him in nearly five years, since I left Korea to start working in London. I mean, I was fourteen and he was eighteen when we left the US, the last time we lived together. It was around the time he was telling me to shut up for singing obnoxiously in the car. "Umma, he's telling me to shut up," I remember moaning. I kept singing, even louder. "I told you to shut up," he said. Then before I could pull back, he spat out the piece of gum he was chewing and stuck it on the top of my head. When we got home, my mom had to chop off a strand of hair, and I had to go around with a tuft sticking out. That's basically where we left things.

So, I invited Tyra to this reunion.

"Are you sure?" she asked. "Don't you want to catch up with him?" Most people found it weird that my brother and I barely spoke to each other.

I insisted Tyra come, and I made it out to my brother that it felt rude excluding my friend who was hosting me.

Tyra and I arrived early to the Thai restaurant he had chosen near where his team was staying. As we waited, I wondered, *Do I hug him, do I not? Will he sit next to me or Tyra? What will we talk about?*

I don't think there was a hug when he arrived. He sat next to me, and we talked about what everyone was doing in Stockholm and what a coincidence it was. It also happened to be his thirty-second birthday that day.

Tyra's eyes darted left and right as my brother and I turned to speak to each other. "You guys look quite different," she said. Everyone always said that when we were younger.

Our lives had also taken such different paths. He was still coaching *Dota 2*, though had moved teams by this time. I remembered him playing computer games back in America but didn't know anything about the esports world.

"It's a winner-takes-all sport," my brother explained. The prize money for the main championship was millions of dollars. Everyone else went home empty-handed.

"How do you do it?" I asked. "I don't think I could ever do what you do." As much as I hated my predictable nine-to-five corporate job, I couldn't imagine his way of life. He'd always been much more of a risk-taker.

When our mains arrived—Tyra and I ordered Thai curries, and my brother ordered a fried rice and tom yum soup—I was reminded of our time in Malaysia. He was never satisfied ordering just one dish.

"I miss the food in Malaysia," he said just then, almost reading my mind. The first thing my brother had done after being discharged from the military was to visit Malaysia for the food.

There was so much I wanted to ask him. Although we looked different and our lives had turned out differently, we had so much in common. As well as our shared genes, we had lived in the same countries at the same time under the same roof. Of course, there were important differences too. For one, he's the eldest; I'm the youngest. He's a boy; I'm a girl. He spent the first few years of his life in Portugal and Rwanda; I spent mine in Korea and the US. His adolescence was in Malaysia and the US; mine was split between the US, Korea and France. But I wished we could at least compare notes. What did he make of our global upbringing? What was the most difficult move for him? Did he feel maladjusted as an adult? Had he suffered from depression?

Instead, we talked about our other halves. I told my brother about Henry, and he told me about someone he was seeing. I think he may have even asked for advice. Tyra politely took a backseat in the conversation to allow the two estranged siblings to reconnect. She later told me that it was like watching two people on a blind date, trying to figure out where their similarities ended and differences began.

After the plates were cleared, Tyra excused herself to go to the bathroom. *Oh no, please don't leave us here*, I thought. Both my brother and I are fluent in English, but we reverted to Korean because that was our language. Thankfully, Tyra wasn't long in the bathroom.

"Happy birthday again," I said at the end of the evening, and wondered how long it would be before I saw my brother again.

31

I didn't speak to my dad for nearly two years after my graduation. On some level it was meant as punishment, not letting him see his daughter again—he didn't deserve it—but I also simply wasn't ready to.

"But he's your father," my mom would say. I knew she missed her own father. Though she would try to protect the image I held of him as the doting grandpa, her father had also been deeply flawed as a parent and as a husband. Still, she missed him and didn't want me to have any regrets. I'd already missed my dad's sixtieth.

"I don't care. It's his loss," I said. But deep down, I knew it was mine too.

The thing is, I am just like my dad in so many ways, both big and small, good and bad. According to Genetics 101, you get 50 percent of your genes from your mother and 50 percent from your father, but it would seem I got a disproportionate number from my dad. My dad is naturally tan and enjoys the sun; my mom is fair and burns easily. My dad has terrible eyesight—he's worn glasses for so long, his face looks misshapen without them; my mom has 20/20 vision. My dad has pudgy hands that look like inflated rubber gloves; my mom has slender fingers and feet so elegant they're admired by shoe store assistants. In all these ways, I am just like my dad. (My brother is the exact opposite and just like my mom.)

The similarities between me and my dad extend beyond our physical attributes. We are both introverted, hyper-organized and obsessed with our routines. We like to plan everything to the minutest detail and triple-check everything is in order. I have always felt that our general temperament and predispositions are similar, especially our heightened sensitivity to caffeine, noises and smells. We even share mannerisms, like the way we scrunch our faces when we are concentrating.

So, one of the meanest things my mom could say to me growing up was, "You're just like your father." She used it sparingly for when she was really upset with me, but when she did, it stung. Because whether it's down to my genes or environment, nature or nurture—no doubt a complex function of both—and whether I like it or not, I am just like him.

~

As unlikely as it seemed on the night of my graduation, my feelings towards my dad mellowed over time, and I was ready to see him again. So I took Henry to visit my parents in Paris over the Easter break in 2019. I had warned Henry about my dad—I didn't tell him everything that happened on my graduation day but enough for him to get a sense— and wondered whether he'd see for himself what my dad was like. I hoped not.

My parents picked us up at Gare du Nord and my dad

and I greeted each other awkwardly, as usual. We acted as if nothing had happened. (I don't know if my mom told him about my suicide attempt.) My brother happened to be visiting at the same time, too, so it became a family reunion, the first one in years. To preempt any awkward conversation, I had asked my mom to tell my dad that Henry's father had died of cancer when Henry was young. But at the dinner table the first evening, I could see my dad gearing up for his punchline: "So, Henry, how is your health?" I wanted to kick him. I fretted over how the rest of the long weekend would go, but my dad was on his best behavior, mostly, and I could see he was trying.

The Easter trip went so smoothly overall, Henry and I returned to Paris two months later to watch Roland-Garros. We were sitting in the garden the first afternoon with a bottle of champagne and some canapés.

"I have some news. I'm pregnant," I announced.

My mom's face lit up instantly. I had expected her to be horrified but she was overjoyed even though Henry and I had only been together six months. She looked so deflated when I added, "Just kidding."

"But I got a new job!" I said excitedly. After five years, I left the accounting firm the day I got my permanent residency as I would no longer need visa sponsorship. Given that neither of my parents was familiar with the corporate world, I tried to explain what a private equity firm was and how my role would change. Maybe hinting at the pay rise would impress my dad.

What I got instead was: "Oh? Your old employer must be glad you're finally leaving?"

My mom shot him a look. I felt my throat constricting but didn't know what to say to that.

"No, actually," Henry interjected, "they're very sad Lena is leaving." I thought it was brave of him to stand up to his potential father-in-law, whom he barely knew. Sensing a shift in my mood, my mom suggested my dad retire for the rest of the afternoon.

Even though I was upset, Henry and I were in Paris for the long weekend only, so I tried to keep my spirits up. But when we sat down for dinner that evening, my dad said, "Henry, you've met my son, haven't you? He's a very smart guy. Full marks on his TOEFL, you know." *What the fuck?* Why was he bringing up my brother's TOEFL scores? TOEFL, by the way, stands for Test of English as a Foreign Language, i.e., a test for non-native speakers. What about my SATs? No, why were we even discussing this?

I cried that evening. Henry saw for himself what I'd been warning him about. I wished it could have been different. My mom also came to check on me. I would get so angry whenever she tried to defend my dad, but even she admitted it was malicious this time.

I knew I shouldn't take it personally. Many years before, when my friend Victor told my dad about his first job, his response was: "UBS, huh? You should really be at Goldman Sachs for investment banking." What did my dad know about investment banking and why, why, why couldn't he just pretend to mouth some congratulatory remark?

It is a mystery to me why he keeps saying the things he does. Is he doing it on purpose, or does he really not understand how hurtful his words can be? Why was it so difficult for him to praise me? A simple "well done." Why did he have to put me down or compare me to my brother, so gratuitously? Was this really his way of trying to keep me grounded and humble?

After this incident, I vowed not to speak to my father again. Fool me once, shame on you; fool me twice, shame on me. I was the idiot for hoping he could change. In the fable "The Scorpion and the Frog," a scorpion asks a frog to carry him over a river. The frog is afraid of being stung, but the scorpion argues that if it did so, both would sink and the scorpion would drown. The frog then agrees, but midway across the river the scorpion stings the frog, dooming them both. When asked why, the scorpion points out that it is its nature.

My dad is the scorpion, his own worst enemy. I have accepted that he is unlikely to ever change. There are times when I wish I could be like those daughters who seem to be in thrall of their fathers whatever their faults—like Jeannette Walls in her memoir *The Glass Castle* or Tara Westover in *Educated*. If they can be so loyal to and protective of their fathers, why can't I look past my dad's flaws, which are trifling in comparison? I wish I could be the bigger person. I wish I could brush off his little remarks. *That's just my father, he means well.* But I know I can't let my guard down.

The thing is, I really do know he means well. I know he loves me; he just doesn't know how to express it. I've seen the way he tries to with my brother is by following his esports tournaments closely. My dad has learned everything there is to know about *Dota 2*: not only its very complicated rules, but the name of the teams, players and coaches, any upcoming tournaments, and of course, the prize money. Our family group chat on KakaoTalk (the Korean WhatsApp) is filled with his commentary on the game. It's his way of relating to my brother because he doesn't know how else to. "How are you?" is just a bit much.

My dad is now retired in Korea. Who knows how much time I'll have left with him? There's still so much I don't know. I know very little about his upbringing and close to nothing about his relationship with his father. In fact, I have only ever seen one photo of my grandfather, the headshot used for the ancestral rites. I wonder if knowing about their relationship would enlighten my relationship with my dad. I really want to understand him better, but I need him to understand me better, too, or at least show that he is trying. I know he has a lot of love for me. And I know I do for him too.

32

On the sixth anniversary of the day I arrived in the UK for work, I applied to become a British citizen. I had all my documents ready: payslips, bank statements, degree certificate, letters from employers, the dates of all the countries I'd lived in (with a note explaining "my dad is a diplomat"). I couldn't wait a day longer.

Despite my timely submission, the Home Office predictably took ages, exacerbated by the COVID-19 pandemic. After waiting for months, I called to check on the status of my application, paranoid that the police cautions I'd received at university were causing issues. I was told to wait indefinitely—no details regarding the status of my application could be disclosed—and that others had been waiting for years. How reassuring!

Then, an email arrived inviting me to have my citizenship ceremony.

I stood proud next to the Union Jack, wearing a sequin Ginger Spice dress, though one that covered more than my crotch. I was, after all, standing next to Queen Elizabeth II— her portrait, that is. I invited Henry and his mom, Anna, as my two guests to the ceremony. They sat in two socially distanced chairs on one side of the grand oak-paneled room at the Old Marylebone Town Hall and took photos of me as I repeated after the registrar: "I, Lena Lee, do solemnly, sincerely and truly declare and affirm that on becoming a British Citizen, I will be faithful and bear true allegiance to Her Majesty Queen Elizabeth the Second, her Heirs and Successors, according to law." The affirmation was a mouthful. I tried my best not to "cock it up."

I then took a pledge of loyalty to the United Kingdom, reminding me of the time I didn't know what that "pleja" thing in America was. After the registrar played the first verse of "God Save the Queen" on his phone (we weren't allowed to sing it due to the pandemic), I was finally presented with my certificate of British citizenship.

I was officially a British citizen now, but how British was I?

As part of my permanent residency application, I had to take the Life in the UK Test, twenty-four multiple-choice questions on topics across British history, traditions, religion, sports, arts, government and law. While some questions required only a bit of common sense—*Which of the following is not a British value?* The answer: terrorism—others I doubt could be answered by the average native Brit. *What was the population of the UK in 1901? What is the money limit for the small claims procedure in England and Wales? Who won gold medals in rowing in five consecutive Olympic Games? Under which king did the people unite to defeat the Vikings?* While it was an interesting crash course, I don't think this knowledge is what makes someone British, or even helps with life in the

UK. (The answers, by the way, are: 40 million; £10,000; Steve Redgrave; and Alfred the Great.)

If we're to use language as a barometer, it's more natural for me to now say *loo*, *trainers* and *trousers* than *toilet*, *sneakers* or *pants*, though I still don't say things like *bloody*, *blimey* or *cheers*. My accent sounds decidedly more British—enough for some Americans to think I sound British—though Brits still think I sound American. I am better at hearing accents too. I can probably tell the difference between, say, a Scottish and Welsh accent with 65 percent accuracy and the difference between a posh and working-class one with 80 percent accuracy.

The next obvious marker of national identity must be sports. I have never been a football fan (by football, I mean soccer), so was surprised to find myself rooting passionately for England during the delayed Euro 2020 tournament. I hadn't even heard of the European Championship before but became a nervous wreck watching the penalty shootout against Italy in the final. The ending image of Gareth Southgate comforting Bukayo Saka after he missed the final penalty stayed with me for weeks. But was this really a sign of my patriotic feelings towards England, or was I just rooting for the underdogs? England hadn't won a tournament since 1966. But how I cursed that Italian goalie's long limbs.

Nearly two decades earlier, Korea and Japan jointly hosted the 2002 World Cup, the first to be held in Asia. I was in Korea that summer in between moving from Malaysia to the US. With defending champions France and second favorites Argentina eliminated in the group stage, South Korea controversially reached the semi-finals after beating

Portugal, Italy and Spain. Despite questionable refereeing decisions leading to allegations of corruption, the mood was high in Korea. The team's Dutch coach, Guus Hiddink, became a national hero and later the first-ever person to be granted honorary South Korean citizenship. Ripples of red spread across the country as everyone chanted in unison and clapped inflatable thunder sticks to the beat of the Korean drums. I learned the names of the players—Park Ji-sung, Cha Du-ri, Ahn Jung-hwan—and dressed up as the Red Devils to watch the third-place playoff against Turkey on a jumbo screen with my mom and some family friends. I shouted, "Hwaiting!"—a Konglish cheer based on the Korean pronunciation of "fighting"—and desperately hoped Korea would win.

Although rooting for a national sports team must be indicative of some desire to be part of a whole, to belong, I struggle to identify with feelings of patriotism and nationalism on a more fundamental level. I didn't have many friends in Paris but one friend I made outside of school was Victor, the recipient of my dad's barb about investment banking. He was my mom's friend's son, who was four years older than me and studying at École Polytechnique, one of the prestigious *grandes écoles*. (In Korean, "mom's friend's son" is used as a synonym for those annoyingly accomplished people who are good at everything. Victor was one of those.)

Victor is ethnic Korean (his Korean name is Hoyeong) but was raised his entire life in France. He dresses Parisian and has a strong French accent when he speaks in English. He is proud to speak Korean fluently, unaware of the occasional mistakes he makes. Once I burst out laughing when we were jogging along the Seine and he said "Miss Sunshine" was out. He hadn't outgrown the baby talk—he also says the Korean equivalents of baba and doggie—as the only people he spoke to in Korean were his parents. Still, he preferred everything Korean: Korean food, Korean music, Korean people. He had in his room a life-size Korean flag on a pole, like the one you might find in the presidential office and was resolute that he would fight for Korea should the war resume.

I found his patriotism misplaced. How could he be ready to give his life for a country he'd never even lived in? Maybe he never felt like he belonged in France, his Asian face singling him out. Maybe what he liked was the idea of Korea. I wondered if it was almost easier for him because Korea was like this mythical home. Even today, fighting for one's country—dying for it—is not something I understand. It's not just the way I feel about Korea. I don't think anyone should die for any country.

Including the three years at university, I have now lived in the UK for almost twelve years, surpassing my previous record of nine years in Korea. But no matter how long I live here, I will never feel the same as a British person born and raised in their homeland. If I tell someone I'm British, they will want a further explanation, even if in the most gentle, oblique way. Here, I am seen as a de facto Korean ambassador. As in Norway, I can get away with teaching people how to use chopsticks even when I don't hold them the "right" way. People want to go to Korean restaurants with me so I can give my verdict on how authentic the cuisine is. They treat me as the authority on how things are done in Korea. I explain how "we" celebrate Christmas (or rather, how we don't), how "we" feel about North Korea. I feel a sense of ambassadorial responsibility.

At the same time, I will never feel the same as a Korean person born and raised in Korea.

When I sent photos from my citizenship ceremony to my family in Korea, their response seemed perfunctory, a lukewarm congratulations. They didn't seem to quite understand the significance of it for me. I suppose it may have been bittersweet for my parents to see their daughter pledge allegiance to Her Majesty the Queen in a Union Jack costume, and that just as they were reestablishing their post-retirement lives in Korea, I was putting down my own roots on the other side of the world.

33

I have never wanted children. When I was younger, my mom put this down to age. She reassured me that my maternal instinct would kick in when the time was right, even though I didn't feel like I needed any reassuring. I could see no reason to want children. My dad had worked hard all his life and poured his savings into me and my brother—particularly my Oxford education—only to have a daughter who barely spoke to him. Was it worth it for him? And God, what I put my mom through from the time I was only ten and didn't speak to her for three months; that would only be the start. In my mind, nothing could possibly make the costs of having children, financial or otherwise, "worth" it.

There are also so many things I want to do—like traveling, reading, maybe even writing another book—that I don't want children interfering with. Some people might consider this selfish, but the way I see it, it's more selfish to have children because you want to propagate your genes and family name. Because you want the experience of raising children. Because you want another chance to vicariously fulfil your dreams. Because you want purpose and meaning in your life.

Perhaps the most fundamental reason for not wanting children, though, was my own experience of depression and wishing I hadn't been born. It was such a dark time there was nothing anyone, not even my mom, could do to fix it—fix me. My heart breaks when I think about what a hard time I gave her with my depression, a daughter telling her mother she doesn't want to live anymore. But the fact is, I can't guarantee a happy world for my child, especially with all the problems they will inevitably face, not least climate change.

My stance was unwavering until I met Henry. Henry has always wanted children. Even though I made it clear to him from our first date that I didn't want them, I softened over time to "Maybe when the time is right." I don't ever want to have children *for* Henry, nor would he want that, but as my friend put it, "You couldn't see yourself having children with anyone until Henry."

Henry and I joke that we will have the most beautiful babies, though we can't imagine what they will look like. Henry is blond and blue-eyed. I feel the need to warn him that our babies are more likely to look like me than him. I don't want him to feel disappointed in case he dreamed of having little kids who looked just like him.

Now that I'm thirty-two years old, I've had to think more about how I might want to raise these hypothetical children. But first, when I give birth, I'd like to have the seaweed soup traditionally eaten postpartum in Korea, as my mom did when she had me. I'd like to find a two-syllable name that is easy to pronounce in both Korean and

English, like mine. I'd like to give a *dol* party. Will they grab the pen like I did? (I've heard that some parents nowadays will even display a stethoscope or gavel in the hope their children will become a doctor or lawyer; others will place a microphone or a football.)

There are so many questions I don't have the answers to. Should I speak to my children in Korean or English? They would become naturally bilingual if I spoke in Korean and Henry in English. And Korean might be more natural for me because that is literally my mother tongue, the language in which my mom spoke to me. But I worry. Nowadays I only ever speak in Korean to my family, which is not that often, and I still find the Korean language awkward, especially for the simplest phrases like *thank you, how are you, I love you*. I feel my relationship with my own parents could be so different if we spoke in English, and don't want my children feeling the same way about me. It's not worth sacrificing good communication, and thus a good relationship, with my children for the sake of their being multilingual. I also remember how I pretended not to speak Korean at my middle school in America. On the other hand, if I stick to English, will they come to resent me as they seek to understand their roots?

What would I cook at home? Lately I've been craving Korean food—bulgogi, bibimbap, bossam, japchae, but especially kimchi, more so than ever before. Is this some reversion to my primal taste, my undeniable Koreanness? I remember when I was younger, my mom and aunts would dedicate a day to making kimchi in giant plastic vats at my grandparents'. These days, I have to make do with store-bought kimchi, but I want to learn to make proper kimchi. I want to cook Korean food at home, but I also remember how embarrassed I was as an adolescent in the US. How would they feel?

I don't even want to start thinking about their education. Based on my experience, I would never want to put them through the Korean education system or a boarding school, but Henry also went to a boarding school and had a very different experience, where he was given freedom, space and autonomy as a student. All I know is that I want them to grow up with a love of learning (forget exams!—though maybe don't tell them I said that).

Every parent wants the best for their children. I know my parents did their best for me and my brother but the way they had to raise us was so different from their own upbringing in Korea. I am sure I will do my best for my children too, but I worry that I'll be ill-equipped to raise a mixed-race child—a "mixed-blood" child in Korean—whose experiences will be so different from my own. I guess all I can do is give it my best, and a lot of love.

～

Over the years and across many moves, I have managed to accumulate a lot of stuff: birthday cards, diaries, farewell letters, love letters, sticker photos, name badges, a Nokia slide phone, yearbooks, notes exchanged during class. Most of the time, these sit idle in cardboard boxes but every now and again—like when I'm trying to write a memoir—they come to life like the toys in *Toy Story*.

I variously wept, laughed and cringed (a lot of cringing, actually) as I went through these items. I was embarrassed to open diaries of my childish outpourings, surprised by photos of me looking way younger than I remember feeling at the time and stirred by letters received many years ago. Sometimes I felt sorry for my younger self and wished I could give her a hug; other times I wanted to shake her for being such a brat. But each piece of memorabilia helped keep me honest.

However, although I've tried to be as truthful as possible in writing this book, I recognize that ultimately it is me, as I am today, who is creating a story and imposing a narrative on my past. Determining what goes in and what stays out— who goes in and who stays out—has proven to be much less straightforward than I expected. And by writing, I am crystallizing my memories as they are today, when I'm sure this book would have looked different had I written it ten years ago, or in ten years' time.

Writing my story has been one of the most challenging things I've ever had to do. Well, I didn't *have* to do it, but I'm glad I did. Because as difficult as it was to relive parts of my past, the act of writing has helped me make sense of it. It has forced me to sit down and disentangle the big mess that was my thoughts, feelings and memories and arrange them into words, sentences and paragraphs. In the process, I've had to return to times I desperately wished to move on from, but writing and rewriting about these experiences has strangely given me a healthy sense of detachment from my own past, almost as if it's someone else's life I'm talking about. I can't quite describe it, but it has been healing.

Part of the motivation for writing this book was for my future children to know that I had a life in the thirty-plus years prior to their arrival. I wasn't born a mother. I wish I had a better sense of this with my own mom when I was growing up.

Until my dad retired in 2019, my mom had been a trailing spouse her entire adult life. But self-absorbed as I was, I only ever thought of her as a mother and not as a human being with her own history, desires, emotions and ambitions. I didn't wonder how my mom found all our moves, what was most difficult for her, or if she missed Korea.

In a rare moment of vulnerability, my mom told me she felt like a failure, for being "just" a housewife. She compared herself to some of her friends who had doctorates and were teaching at universities or running their own businesses. She didn't say this in a resentful because-of-you-kids or even because-of-my-husband way, but I was sad to hear it. I had no idea she felt like that.

When I asked her what she would have liked to have become, my mom said a psychologist or an anthropologist, which is so apt because she loves people and culture. She immersed herself in each country we lived in, learning the language and culture and making local friends, lots of them. In my mind, my mom is a true ambassador for Korea. Anyone who's been fortunate enough to meet her will have been left with a more favorable impression of Korea, as well as having a good friend.

My mom was incredulous when I tried to explain her own achievements to her. "You really think so?" she asked.

"Most definitely."

~

When I was depressed, my mom told me to have faith that there'd be a day when I would be smiling again. That day has come—yes, Umma, you were right—though I don't take that for granted. Although I haven't been depressed since 2018, I don't consider myself "cured," partly for fear of tempting fate. At the same time, neither does depression feel inevitable like it once did. For me, the fact that I'm not wishing I was dead is progress I couldn't have imagined at the time. So, it's important to me that I appreciate each day that I'm not depressed. If anything, I believe my experience of depression has given me a heightened appreciation for life. I feel grateful to be alive.

While there's a lot in my past I regret, a lot of things I wish I could have done differently, I no longer want to feel shame. I no longer want to feel ashamed of my mental health issues, whether that's my depression, drinking, binge-eating or suicidal thoughts. As the renowned addiction expert Dr. Gabor Maté put it, the question we need to ask is not why the addiction, but why the pain. I want to be kind to myself, and proud of myself.

Oh, and if anyone asks me where I am from, I will refer them to this book, the slightly longer version of, "I'm Korean, but…"

Note to the Reader

Please review this book!

Dear reader, thank you so much for picking up my book. If you enjoyed *Girl Uprooted*, please consider leaving a short review on Amazon and/or Goodreads. Even a few sentences would be greatly appreciated as reviews help authors more than you might think.

Say hello!

Connect with me on Instagram @thelenalee or visit my website: www.thelenalee.com

Acknowledgements

Thank you, thank you, thank you:

To my friends, for always being there for me, and making me believe in friendships again. You guys mean the world to me.

To old friends and boyfriends, for their generous support and permission to share my memories. Reconnecting with you has been most heartwarming and unexpectedly healing.

To Ruth Van Reken, David Pollock and Michael Pollock for their book *Third Culture Kids*, an invaluable resource for anyone growing up multiculturally. It was in this book that I first came across the concept of unresolved grief. Ruth, thank you so much for your support with this book and everything you have done for TCKs around the world.

To Alex Eccles for his incisive editorial feedback which, for all intents and purposes, became my "bible" as I revised draft after draft. To Aliya Gulamani at Unbound for her support of writers of color. I feel honored to have made the inaugural Unbound Firsts shortlist in 2022. To Laurie Chittenden for her feedback on an early draft, delivered in the most empathetic and encouraging way.

To my early readers: Dee, Rachel, Shreya, Sabi and Abhi.

Thank you so much for looking out for me and making me feel so safe. All your feedback has been incredibly helpful.

To my brother, who read this book in one sitting, then shared his own experiences of growing up around the world with me. I'm so glad that we got to compare notes at last and connect on a deeper level.

To my parents. Umma, thank you for supporting me with this book, which I know wasn't easy for you to read. Please know that I feel exceptionally privileged to be your daughter. Appa, thank you for all your sacrifices. I wish it was easier for me to say this in person.

To Henry, for his infinite patience and support throughout all the ups and downs of my writing and publishing this book. I couldn't have done this without you. Thank you, Big Koo. I love you.

References

Chapter 29

Oishi, S. & Schimmack, U. (2010). Residential Mobility, Well-Being, and Mortality. *Journal of Personality and Social Psychology*, 98 (6), 980–994.

Webb, R.T., Pedersen, C.B. & Mok, P.L.H. (2016). Adverse Outcomes to Early Middle Age Linked With Childhood Residential Mobility. *American Journal of Preventive Medicine*, 51 (3), 291–300.

Werkman, S., Farley, G.K., Butler, C. & Quayhagen, M. (1981). The Psychological Effects of Moving and Living Overseas. *Journal of the American Academy of Child Psychiatry*, 20 (3), 645–657.